# POPULAR EDUCATION IN
# EIGHTEENTH CENTURY ENGLAND

# POPULAR EDUCATION
# IN
# EIGHTEENTH CENTURY
# ENGLAND

VICTOR E. NEUBURG

THE WOBURN PRESS : LONDON

First published by

WOBURN BOOKS LIMITED

10 Woburn Walk, London WC1 0JL

Copyright © 1971 V. E. Neuburg

ISBN 0 7130 0000 7

*Printed in Great Britain by*
*Stephen Austin and Sons Ltd., Hertford.*

# CONTENTS

# ACKNOWLEDGMENTS

Gratitude is due to Barbara Gilbert for her invaluable and constant initiative in the transformation of a University thesis into the present book. Without her the task would have been impossible, and I should not have attempted it alone.

To Professor G.H. Bantock, my appreciation of his encouragement; and to my wife and daughter, who have lived with the eighteenth century for so long, my thanks for their understanding.

Finally, I am indebted to the many Librarians and others responsible for books and archives — too numerous to mention — who have never failed to respond to my queries.

V.E.N.

# Chapter 1

## TOWARDS A THEORY OF POPULAR EDUCATION

In England in the second half of the twentieth century the fact of a mass reading public is very much taken for granted. For very nearly one hundred years we have had a system of compulsory elementary education which has done much to make universal literacy a reality. The origins of mass readership, however, lie further back in history than the Education Act of 1870 would suggest; and the existence of a popular literature which was well established and widely diffused at least one hundred years earlier prompts the present study, which is concerned with finding a preliminary answer to the question: To what extent was the ability to read a common achievement amongst working men and women in eighteenth century England?

This was a period of profound and far-reaching changes in English life. ". . . The middle years of the eighteenth century", wrote Dorothy George, "are a watershed dividing old England from the modern world as we know it."[1] It was the rise of the factory system which heightened the contrast between old and new. Through its creation of new pressures in society, some of which led to the making of the working class, it provides a context in which growth of the ability to read can be traced and evaluated.

There was no real theory of popular education at this time; simply a desultory debate over whether children of the poor should be taught to read or not. The points of view of those who held that they should, and those who maintained the converse, were rooted in an identical social theory which saw society as a divinely ordered mechanism in which everyone knew his place, and the primary concern of both sides was to maintain the established order. Those who opposed popular education did so on the grounds that

1. M. D. George, *England in Transition*, 1962.

1

it would eventually destroy a society which was based upon rigid social distinctions; thus the only way to preserve it was to deny education to the poor. The motive of the reformers was a charitable one: to modify the ignorance of the poor so that they might read the Scriptures and earn a useful though humble living, grateful to their superiors and always conscious of a duty to them. In this way, it was thought, the continuance of existing social patterns would be ensured.

With this common acceptance, then, of a pattern of society whose values were symbolised by the terms rank, station, duty and decorum[2], the divergence of opinion concerned the effect which educational provision for the poor, even of the most scanty kind, would have upon such a society. So far as existing records make it possible, an examination of the extent of this provision will be made in the following pages; and this may enable some judgment to be made of the aptness of the description "scanty". Briefly, the elementary instruction which was available, and by means of which boys and girls from labouring families learned their letters, was provided in one of two ways: by "dame schools", which were entirely independent enterprises requiring no standard of skill or experience whatever on the part of those who taught in them; or in "Charity" schools, or "Free" schools, which came into being as a result of the philanthropic impetus which inspired reform movements during the eighteenth century.

Outstanding among these movements was the Society for Promoting Christian Knowledge. Founded in 1699, it had almost at once turned its attention to the task of educating poor children in the charity schools which it initiated all over the country. Some minimum standards were laid down for those appointed to teach in these schools, but in the main these reflected the fundamental objective, as stated in the Society's "Orders", of providing "the Education of

---

2. cf. John Mason: "A man that knows himself will deliberately consider and attend to the particular Rank and Station in which Providence hath placed him; and what is the Duty and Decorum of that station". *Self-Knowledge*, 10th Ed., 1778.

Poor Children in the Knowledge and Practice of the Christian Religion".

The Methodist movement was, of course, one which exerted considerable influence in the eighteenth century; but it made comparatively little direct contribution either to the provision of schools where reading was taught, or to the discussion which lay behind such endeavours. Later in the century it turned with enthusiasm to the cause of popular education, but initially its concern was more for the salvation and reform of the adult.

Among outright opponents of the idea of charity schools was Bernard de Mandeville, author of the *Fable Of The Bees*, which included in its 2nd Edition in 1723 an "Essay on Charity and Charity-Schools". At the outset he draws a distinction between charity and pity, and contends that schools were the result of the latter emotion. His argument is both verbose and digressive; but briefly, the points he makes are that (a) the poor do not need any education; (b) if they have learning, they become too proud to work; (c) education makes servants claim higher wages while at the same time they do not want to do servile work; (d) though it might be reasonable to teach reading, the teaching of writing cannot possibly be justified. De Mandeville's thesis was a sociological and economic one: no nation can be great without vast numbers of ignorant people to do the drudgery.

In the seventeen-fifties, Soame Jenyns asserted that like the lower animals in their bliss, so, in their inferior way, the poor are happy too. Ignorance is their opiate, "a cordial administered by the gracious hand of providence"[3]; and from this followed the argument that it ill behoved men to frustrate this benevolent purpose by an "ill judged and improper education".

Towards the end of the century George Hadley wrote an attack upon the provision of education for the poor which is notable not for any new ideas, but rather for the force with which the older ones were re-stated. Of all unlikely places, it appeared in his *A New And Complete History*

3. *Free Enquiry into the Nature and Origin of Evil*, 1757.

... *Of The Town Of Kingston-Upon-Hull,* which was published in 1788, and was occasioned by a consideration of the local Sunday Schools. So far as these institutions promoted attendance at a place of worship, and decent behaviour, Hadley approved of them; but instruction in reading was a different matter. "By diffusing the knowledge of reading", he wrote, "we shall enlarge the minds of the vulgar; — True, but does it necessarily follow, that the lower classes will become more industrious, more virtuous, more happy? Certainly not."

He goes on to develop an argument reminiscent of Bernard de Mandeville's earlier essay:

"The working poor, are by far the most numerous class of people, and when kept in due subordination, they compose the riches of the nation. But there is a degree of ignorance necessary to keep them so, and to make them either useful to others or happy in themselves. What ploughman who could read the renowned history of Tom Hickathrift, Jack the Giant-Killer, or the Seven Wise Men, would be content to whistle up one furrow and down another, from dawn in the morning, to the setting of the sun?"

The evils which will result if reading is widespread are not only that minds will be damaged by "monstrous and alluring improbabilities", but also that men will teach themselves to write, and the twin evils of reading and writing can only lead to the depravity of the poor, who might otherwise remain industrious labourers.

Antagonism to education for the poor persisted into the nineteenth century, and the arguments put forward changed little. Mr. Davies Giddy, M. P., in a House of Commons debate in 1807, said:

"... Giving education to the labouring classes of the poor ... would be prejudicial to their morals and happiness; it would teach them to despise their lot in life, instead of making them good servants in agriculture and other laborious employments. Instead of teaching them subordination, it would render them fractious and refractory."

Those who supported Giddy's view must have felt that the French Revolution added great strength to their arguments; and it is interesting to note that de Mandeville, Jenyns and Giddy all sensed the *power* to affect society that was implicit in mass literacy, and reacted against proposals for any extension of education by arguing that the status quo could only be maintained if the poor were kept in ignorance.

A final example remains to be quoted from a writer who held that education indiscriminately bestowed was a general evil; and although the book in which these views appeared was published in 1828, the argument in fact differed very little from that advanced by Bernard de Mandeville about one hundred years before. In *Something New Or Men And Manners, A Critique On The Follies And Vices Of The Age*, which appeared anonymously, the author, Mrs. Lucy Hake, has an essay "On the Education of the Poor" in which, with a somewhat heavy humour, she deplores the spread of education amongst the "lower class" as tending to distract their minds from habits of industry:

> "The labourers' children are no longer taught to know or mend a stocking, to sharpen knives or brush a coat – no – they must away to school to learn to read and write."

Mrs. Hake did express a grudging praise for some of the education societies of the early nineteenth century, under whose provision "so many thousands of the poor and needy are taught at any trifling expense". Yet she points out that these establishments fail in one important respect: the poor are not taught to work hard, and the result, calamitous to society at large, is idleness which tends to an increase of crime.

Her comments would not be of especial interest if they did not show how prejudice remained strong in the face of a movement towards education for all which was beginning to gather momentum at the very time when she was setting down her objections to it; and the arguments she uses are those of the eighteenth century.

Certainly no desire to "distract their minds from habits of industry" entered into the motives of the reformers of this period. Their efforts were a practical expression of that growing sense of philanthropy which saw Christian endeavour in the field of education as an answer to the problems of ignorance, but equally as an important element in the promotion of an ordered Christian society in which a pious and hard-working labouring class was content with its lot. Griffith Jones, in *Welch Piety*, 1742, expressed this attitude succinctly:

"It is but a cheap education that we would desire for them (i.e. the poor), only the moral and religious branches of it, which indeed is the most necessary and indispensable part. The sole design of this charity is to inculcate upon such . . . as can be prevailed on to learn, the knowledge and practice, the principles and duties of the Christian Religion; and to make them good people, useful members of Society, faithful servants of God, and men and heirs of eternal life."

In practice, this meant instruction in reading the Bible[4]; but the most revealing part of Jones' statement is his use of the words "we" and "them", which underlines the view taken by the most advanced of the reformers that such education was intended to perpetuate the social order, and was in no sense at all regarded as an instrument of social change. Current assumptions about the nature of society were never at any time called into question by those who sought education for the poor.

Joseph Butler, Bishop of Bristol, in *A Sermon Preached In The Parish Church Of Christ-Church, London* (London, 1745) said:

"It is most manifest that a Christian and useful Education to the children of the Poor is very necessary to their Piety, Virtue and honest Livelihood."

He was at some pains to point out, however, that children

---

4. See for example R. T. Jenkins, *A Conspectus of Griffith Jones Schools in North Wales, 1738-1761,* The Bulletin of the Board of Celtic Studies, Vol. V, Part 4, May, 1931.

were *not* to be educated in order to remove them from the station of life into which they had been born, and his phrase "a Christian and useful education" epitomised eighteenth century sentiments regarding education for the poor. Together with his prescient remarks about the significance of the printed word, Bishop Butler's sermon makes a notable contribution to the somewhat sparse educational literature of the period.

"Charity-Children", wrote W. Hendley, "are taught to do their Duty in that State of Life, into which it shall please God to call them". In *A Defence of the Charity-Schools*, 1735, Hendley showed himself an enthusiastic supporter of such institutions, and his book is a forthright answer to de Mandeville's arguments for keeping the poor in ignorance.

James Nelson, an apothecary, believed that education should be adapted to the class in which the child was born[5]. He distinguished five classes in English society: Nobility, Gentry, Genteel Trades (i.e. those requiring large capital), Common Trades, Peasantry. In his general remarks about the nature of education, Nelson is at some pains to emphasise the need for guidance in reading, and he speaks of "the swarms of lewd Plays, Poems and Romances, calculated to inflame the Minds and corrupt the Hearts of the Readers". A lack of discrimination can vitiate the whole purpose of education which ought to make children "wise and good".

So far as the education of the poor is concerned, he defines the class of society he is discussing and then suggests a suitable curriculum:

"I ... now proceed to treat of a fourth (i.e. class of people); which comprehends a very large Part of the Kingdom, but London particularly; viz all the inferior Trades and many others ... Men very valuable in their Way, and of boundless Use to Society; tho' by the Wisdom of Providence born rather to Labour than to Idleness; to be obedient to the Laws, than to be Dispensers of them."

5. *An Essay on the Government of Children*, 1756.

For these people reading, writing, arithmetic, drawing and a knowledge of maps are sufficient – by eighteenth century standards this was a fairly ambitious scheme, and the teaching of writing, less common than instruction in reading, is justified in these words:

"Every Man who is acquainted with Life must daily see the too general Defects of Hand-writing. If a Bricklayer, or any other Workman, brings in a Bill, what a pitiful Figure it makes; nay it is sometimes so bad that none but the Writer himself can read it."[6]

Girls of this class should be taught simply reading, writing and elementary arithmetic; and then the author turns his attention to the lowest class of all:

". . . the lowest class of people in London particularly. These People possess indeed the Ignorance of the Peasants, but seldom equal them in Innocence. Many are abandoned in every Vice; many indeed are honest and industrious; but even among those who are themselves good, their Children, thro' an early false Fondness, or the Corruption of others, are usually ignorant, untoward and vicious. Whence we daily see and hear in the open Streets such things as are insults on Mankind."

A more restricted curriculum, consisting of reading, writing and elementary arithmetic, is recommended for boys of this class, while girls are to be taught simply reading and needlework. These subjects, thinks the author, should go some way towards reforming these children.

Nelson's theories of education are based upon the accepted view of society, and his ideas are typical. An earlier writer who had also made some distinction between the education appropriate for the rural and for the urban poor was Isaac Watts in *An Essay Towards the Encouragement of Charity Schools,* 1728. Watts held that the ability to read the Bible was essential to an understanding of

6. The assumption here that bricklayers or other workmen could write at all is an interesting one. cf. G. Sturt, *The Wheelwright's Shop,* Cambridge, 1948, p. 4. A bricklayer and a tallow chandler sign a conveyance in 1721.

religion, and that poor children should receive instruction in reading for two or three hours each day. With regard to writing he was less certain, and the expression of his reservations led him to distinguish between various educational needs, and to question the utility of teaching every child to write:

"I will by no means contend for writing as a Matter of equal Necessity or Advantage with that of Reading ... And there may also be some of the Poor who dwell in very obscure Villages, and are confined to rural Labours, and others in Towns or Cities, and especially Girls, whose Business is most within Doors at Home, who may have but very little Occasion, and as little Inclination to use a Pen. I would not therefore by any means have it made a necessary Part of a Charity-School, that the Children should be taught to write."

Watts was inclined to think that reading was sufficient for country children: "The Poor who are bred in Towns and Cities, should enjoy some small Advantages in their Education, beyond those who are born in far distant Fields and Villages".

Writing later in the century, George Chapman, who was Master of the Grammar School in Dumfries, contributed a great deal to the theory influencing the growing activity in the field of education for the poor. He was author of *A Treatise on Education,* which was first published in Edinburgh in 1773 and reprinted several times, and he makes recommendations for the education of this class, whom he describes thus:

" ... those who are destined for employments which require bodily strength, such as labourers, servants, and the greatest part of manufacturers, need not a very extensive education. It may be enough if they can be taught to read the English language, and to write. To this should be added psalmody, and perhaps the most useful rules of arithmetic. In this manner should they be employed at school."

Chapman goes on to suggest that health should be a matter of concern for parents and teachers, and that the curriculum should include exercise, under supervision, corresponding to the way of life for which the pupils are destined, to act as a kind of easy preparation for the labouring tasks which will be their lot. This, he claims, will prevent the formation of habits of idleness, and there will be a greater willingness to work hard.

"... to reconcile the lowest classes of mankind to the fatigues of constant labour, and otherwise mortifying thoughts of a servile employment, pains should be taken to convince them, when young, that subordination is necessary in society; that they ought to submit to their masters or superiors in every thing that is lawful; that nature has formed us for action; that happiness does not consist in indolence, nor in the possession of riches ... but in habits of industry and contentment, in temperance and frugality; in the consciousness of doing our duty in the station in which we are placed."

In order that the poor should procure good will and assistance, they must be benevolent and obliging; strong passions are to be avoided at all times; and the virtues which should characterise them are humility; meekness; forgiveness; gratitude; self-denial; submission to the will, and obedience to the law, of God. If they conform to this pattern, then they are entitled to the meagre educational provision quoted above. One proviso is made with regard to boys of exceptional talent — such pupils, says Chapman, should not be barred from a liberal education, and are in fact to be educated at public expense.

George Chapman's views are reproduced with a great deal of fidelity in *The Shepherd of Salisbury Plain,* one of Hannah More's[7] "Cheap Repository Tracts", which were written at the suggestion of John Porteus, Bishop of London, to counteract the secular popular literature of the day, and also to act as an antidote to the radical writings of Thomas Paine.[8] They came out between 1795 and 1798, were widely circulated and subsequently reprinted.

7. See M. G. Jones, *Hannah More*, Cambridge, 1952.
8. His *Rights of Man* was first published in 1791.

Chapman's book went through four editions between 1773 and 1790, and since Hannah More was interested in a wide range of educational problems, it seems probable that she read this popular manual which was first published when she was twenty-eight.

Possibly, too, she was influenced in her attempt to provide cheap religious reading matter for the poor by the views of Joseph Butler, Bishop of Bristol, expressed in his *Sermon* of 1745 already referred to. Butler realised more clearly than most of the earlier writers on education the implications of the printed word for society. He pointed out that children should be taught to read so that they could read the Bible, and also so that they could earn a living. As a result of the spread of printing:

> "Knowledge has been increased, and some sort of litera-ture is become general. And if this be a Blessing, we ought to let the Poor, in their Degree, share it with us."

Bishop Butler goes on to urge "People of Rank" not to delude themselves into thinking that ignorance will keep the lower classes more dutiful or servile. Reading, he says, will surely lead to an improvement in moral and religious knowledge, and the feeling for religion can be kept up by the distribution of suitable religious books amongst the poor.

Certainly he had anticipated Hannah More's views regarding the importance of cheap books and the signifi-cance of the printed word. The French Revolution had made the danger from revolutionary and atheistic books appear a pressing one in her day, but the general sentiments expressed by Bishop Butler are undoubtedly those that she would have approved. The book mentioned above, *The Shepherd of Salisbury Plain,* illustrates her view of what education ought to do for the pious and deserving poor. It was widely distributed, and was reprinted right through the nineteenth century.

As the story opens, Mr. Johnson, "a very worthy, chari-table gentleman", is travelling across Salisbury Plain when he meets a shepherd who is described in terms reminiscent of Wordsworth:

". . . Mr. Johnson was not more struck with the decency of his mean and frugal dress, than with his open, honest countenance, which bore strong marks of health, cheerfulness and spirit."

He enters into conversation with the shepherd, who loses no time in making clear to Mr. Johnson that "I only submit to the lot that is appointed me", and he goes on to express his gratitude to God for having allowed him to be poor, and so exposed to fewer temptations than he would be if he were rich. Even more revealing, perhaps, is the fragment of autobiography with which the shepherd regales his hearer:

". . . blessed be God! Through his mercy I learned to read when I was a little boy; though reading was not so common when I was a child as I am told, through the goodness of Providence and the generosity of the rich, it is likely to become nowadays. I believe there is no day, for the last thirty years, that I have not peeped at my Bible. If he can't find time to read a chapter, I defy any man to say he can't find time to read a verse."

The shepherd, with his wife and eight children, lives in a cottage with two rooms, and earns 1s. per day. His wife is in poor health; but in spite of this, the children are brought up to habits of piety, industry and frugality.

Mr. Johnson gives the shepherd a crown, and continues his journey "more disposed to envy than pity the shepherd", whose home he resolves to visit upon his return across Salisbury Plain. This he does a few days later, and arrives just as the family is about to eat its frugal Sunday dinner consisting of potatoes and a piece of coarse loaf. No meat had been purchased with Mr. Johnson's gift, as the money was owed to the doctor, and next to sin, nothing was worse than debt; in any case, a good dinner was not worthy to be compared with a contented mind.

Eventually the village clerk dies, and the shepherd is appointed to succeed him, moving into his cottage. Mr. Johnson sets up a parish Sunday School of which the shepherd is appointed master, and his wife becomes mistress of a "Small Weekly School" in which she teaches ten or a dozen girls knitting, sewing, spinning and other useful ways of earning their living. The salary is moderate, for, says Mr. Johnson, "I am not going to make you rich, but useful".

The shepherd's reply to this remark illustrates clearly the kind of sentiment amongst the poor that educationalists wanted to foster and strengthen as a bastion against thoughts of revolution and social disturbance:

> ". . . 'Not rich, sir?', cried the shepherd. 'How can I ever be thankful enough for such blessings? . . . Indeed my cup runs over with blessings; I hope God will give me humility.' Here he and Mary (his wife) looked at each other and burst into tears."

Tales of this kind represented an avowed attempt to counteract what were considered to be the dangerous and pernicious effects of chapbooks and political pamphlets.[9] Hannah More was not the first reformer to try to reach the poor with cheap improving books, but she was in a very important sense a great innovator in that she provided cheap fiction with recognisable working class characters. The Society for Promoting Christian Knowledge, and the Methodists, were issuing religious tracts which made no concession at all to the tastes and background of the audience for whom they were intended; Hannah More, on the other hand, with a unique blend of evangelical theory and practical experience, issued cheap "improving" literature which looked exactly like the very simple secular publications which had formed virtually the sole reading matter of the poor. Her books were always well written, and the characters clearly drawn. She was aware of the opposition aroused by proposals for elementary education of the poor; and nowhere is this more clearly shown than in one of her tracts, *The Sunday School.* Mrs. Jones, who is soliciting subscriptions for the foundation of a village Sunday School, is told by Farmer Hoskins:

> ". . . I will give nothing; hoping it will spur on the rest to refuse. Of all the foolish inventions, and new-fangled devices to ruin the country, that of teaching the poor to read is the very worst."

9. See for example W. Jones, *The Jubilee Memorial of the Religious Tract Society,* London, 1850.

Mrs. Jones replies:

". . . And I, farmer, think that to teach good principles to
the lower classes is the most likely way to save the country. Now in order to do this, we must teach them to read."

Certainly there were critics of Hannah More — William
Hone wrote in strong terms of the "dull lying consolation"
she offered to the starving poor; and yet it is a proof of the
enduring quality of her tracts that he was making these
attacks twenty years after their first appearance. Amongst
the many supporters Hannah More won for herself was a
minister, schoolmaster and voluminous writer on religious
topics whose books have largely been forgotten. He is recalled now, both as an enthusiastic admirer of Hannah More,
and as almost the last of the eighteenth century writers who
saw the education of the poor as a "pious and useful"
exercise in charity.

John Evans was born in 1767 and died in 1827. He was
related to Caleb Evans, who had been active in the Bristol
Education Society from 1770. In 1795 he opened an
academy in Heston, Middlesex, and later moved to Islington,
where his school prospered until 1825. Apart from his
academy, he was interested in other forms of education. On
the 17th July, 1808, he preached a sermon at Canterbury on
behalf of the Royal Free School, and this was printed in the
same year under the title *The Importance of Educating the
Poor.*

Although published at the outset of the nineteenth century, the argument belongs to the eighteenth. Education of
the poor is declared to be an act of Christian charity which
has also practical results, because the poor man who can read
and write is never the prey of idleness. The importance of
reading is stressed: ". . . it lies at the foundation of everything else".

Evans praises religious tracts, and in particular those of
Hannah More: "Her 'Shepherd of Salisbury Plain' is known
to most of you, it has been the subject of just and general
admiration". It is also pointed out that it is through education that the poor become acquainted with the duties they

owe to society, and the sermon ends with the ringing declaration ". . . I would have every poor child in the nation able to read the Bible!".

John Evans should not be dismissed as simply repeating the stock arguments in favour of education, for in two respects — however fleetingly — he shows a remarkable prescience. Firstly, he refers to "man as a social being" who "stands in need of knowledge, as a ground of mutual enjoyment". Secondly, he refers to the profitable use of leisure spent in "reading rather than riot and dissipation". The use of the word "need" in connection with man as a social being is surprisingly modern; so too is his mention of the use of leisure. These were forward-looking ideas, and they were put forward in support of Evans' unequivocal plea for universal literacy.

In 1791–1792 Thomas Paine, in his *Rights of Man*, outlined proposals for state education; but, interesting as they were, such ideas were so far in advance of their time that they have almost the quality of prophetic writings. Moreover, while Paine's political and religious views generated a good deal of controversy and comment, his views upon education seem to have been ignored, and one looks in vain at the radical literature of the period for books or pamphlets upon educational topics which used Paine's views as a basis for discussion — neither did anyone think it worth while to refute them.

During the last thirty or so years of the eighteenth century many other reformers had written in support of popular education, produced textbooks, and founded schools. The battle was far from won; but public interest in the subject had quickened, and by the nineteenth century the scope and substance of the debate had changed considerably, in that the struggle for the control of education became the central issue in a discussion which became increasingly complex, and not seldom acrimonious.

# Chapter 2

## EDUCATION IN PRACTICE

### I TEACHERS

Eighteenth century writers had very little to say about the teachers of basic subjects, and contemporary comments seem to indicate that these men and women were held in very low esteem. James Talbott, author of *The Christian School-Master* (London, 1707), refers to:

"...those Teachers of a Lower Class, and consequently of Lower Talents, who are Employed to Instruct Poor Children in such Things only, as are most Necessary and Suitable to their Condition."

Another writer remarks that:

"...It is commonly thought so tiresome an Undertaking, to teach Children to Spell and Read English, that a peevish Schoolmaster is not judged to have Patience enough to do it. And, therefore, they are sent to a Mistress, supposing she may be more fit to deal with them in their tender Years; where partly thro' the Ignorance of many such Teachers, and partly Neglect, the Children often spend whole Years to little Advantage."[1]

The writer of a text-book published some years later spoke of "the Business of Laying the Foundation, or First Principles of Learning" as usually falling into "unskilful hands".[2] Solomon Lowe alluded in *The Critical Spelling-Book* to teachers as "dames (many of them in the decay of life, or distress of fortune)"; while later in the century Thomas Sheridan described the teaching of reading in unflattering terms. "This employment", he wrote, "re-

---

1. John Urmston, *The London Spelling-Book*, 4th Ed., London, 1710, Preface.
2. John Collyer, *The General Principles of Grammar Especially Adapted to the English Tongue*, Nottingham, 1735.

quiring no great talents, usually fell to the lot of old women, or men of mean capacities."[3]

There was no recognised method of becoming a teacher; and while it may be an extreme case to cite William Bowker, a dissolute tradesman who became a teacher when his peruke-making business failed in 1748, there are similar illustrations of the fact that teaching was regarded as a job that anyone could drift into. As John Urmston wrote in *A New Help to Accidence* (London, 1710), ". . .it may be Broken Tradesmen, Attornies and Lawyers Clerks, fit for nothing else, that set up for School Masters"; while R. Campbell's *The London Tradesman* of 1747, containing a table of trades with details of entry, apprenticeship, etc., makes no mention of teaching. David Love, who was born in 1750 and had a varied career as miner, soldier, shopkeeper and chapman, wrote in his autobiography that at one stage he was "persuaded by some people in a large village, to keep a school to teach their children. . . .". James Lewis, a relative of Parson Woodforde, became a schoolmaster in Nottingham after he had been wounded in the leg while serving in the Army as a private soldier. When the father of Robert Bloomfield, the poet, died in 1767 his widow, with six children to support, opened a school in order to provide for her family. The father of Thomas Chatterton, the poet, was described as a "dissipated schoolmaster"[4] and the family of Nicholas Manners, the Methodist, had a teacher lodging with them who "though immoral in practice, was a good master, and exceedingly strict in his school discipline".[5]

The scanty references to teachers in the poetry of the period suggest strongly that elementary teaching was a task for old women, for widows, or for the humblest members of society. William Shenstone in his poem "The Schoolmistress" recalls Sarah Lloyd, who ran a dame school which he had attended as a child:

3. *Lectures on the Art of Reading*, 2 vols., London, 1775.
4. H. D. Roberts (Ed.), *The Poems of Thomas Chatterton*, 2 Vols., London, 1906, Vol. 1, p. xiii.
5. *Some particulars of the Life and Experience of Nicholas Manners*, York, 1785.

"In every village, mark'd with little spire,
Embow'r'd in trees, and hardly known to Fame,
There dwells, in lowly shed, and mean attire,
A matron old, whom we school-mistress name;
Who boasts unruly brats with birch to tame.

Her cap, far whiter than the driven snow,
Emblem right meet of decency does yield:
Her apron dy'd in grain, as blue, I trowe
As is the Hare-bell that adorns the field:
And in her hand, for scepter, she does wield
Tway birchen sprays; . . .

Lo now with state she utters the command;
Eftsoons the urchins to their tasks repair;
Their books of stature small they take in hand,
Which with pellucid horn secured are,
To save from finger wet the letters fair:"

Another poet who remembered his first teacher was
Henry Kirk White, born in Nottingham in 1785, who attended
Mrs. Garrington's school from the age of three until five. In
one of his earliest poems, "Childhood", written when he
was fourteen or fifteen, there is a sketch of her:

"The village matron kept her little school,
Gentle of heart, yet knowing well to rule;
Staid was the dame, and modest was her mien;
Her garb was coarse, yet whole, and nicely clean:
Her neatly-border'd cap, as lily fair,
Beneath her chin was pinn'd with decent care;
And pendant ruffles, of the whitest lawn,
Of ancient make, her elbows did adorn.
Faint with old age, and dim were grown her eyes,
A pair of spectacles their want supplies;"

Both Shenstone and Kirk White present a somewhat
sentimentalised view of a teacher based upon their own
memories of early days at school. George Crabbe, on the
other hand, with a shrewdness of observation and sense of
reality that characterise the best of his poetry, is not
content with such a superficial view, and looks beyond it
to mention the social function of the dame school:

"Yet one there is, that small regard to Rule
Or Study pays, and still is deem'd a School;
That, where a deaf, poor, patient Widow sits,
And awes some thirty Infants as she knits;
Infants of humble, busy Wives, who pay
Some trifling Price for Freedom through the day."[6]

Elsewhere in the book Crabbe describes her as "the Poor Widow, who pronounced the alphabet for infants", an indication that she carried out some rudimentary teaching of reading. This impression is made more definite by his recollection of a teacher who had retired, and who lived in very poor circumstances:

"Can I mine antient Widow pass unmov'd?
Shall I not think what pains the Matron took
When first I trembled o'er the gilded Book?
How she, all patient, both at Eve and Morn,
Her Needle pointed at the guarding Horn;
And how she sooth'd me, when with Study sad
I labour'd on to reach the final Zad?"

There is probably an echo here of Crabbe's own early school experiences in East Anglia.

Crabbe referred more than once to the grinding poverty which became the lot of these women when they were no longer able to teach. A tragic description of a retired teacher occurs in "Ellen Orford". After a troubled life during which she bore an idiot daughter and buried three sons, Ellen found happiness in running a school; but her contentment was short-lived, for she went blind and spent the remainder of her life in poverty and patient resignation, loving mankind and confident in the love of God.

The other teachers described by Crabbe were both men. Abel Keene ran a school for poor boys until he was employed by a merchant as a clerk; and Reuben Dixon:

"Poor Reuben Dixon has the noisiest School
Of ragged Lads, who ever bow'd to Rule;
Low in his Price - the Men who heave our Coals
And clean our Causeways, send him Boys in shoals:"

6.  *The Borough*, 3rd Ed., 2 Vols., London, 1810, Vol. 2.

Crabbe's elementary school teachers all come from the poorer classes, and while he does not minimise the importance of the work they do, his portrait of them is a grim one. Both the men he describes are ill suited to their work, and the two women spend their retirement in the most abject poverty. Moreover, except in one case – Ellen Orford – he does not mention the quality of piety which we find stressed by the few writers upon education who discussed the attributes of a successful teacher. "Schoolteachers", George Snell had written in 1649 (*The Right Teaching of Useful Knowledg*), "ought to be of a pious qualitie, of gentle demeanour, of a chois neatness in their person, apparel and gesture, of invincible patience, of unwearied industrie, of a genial delight in teaching. . . .".

Snell was amplifying William Petty's view, published a year earlier, "that the Business of Education be not, as now, committed to the worst and unworthiest of Men, but that it be seriously studied and practised by the best and ablest Persons".[7]

At the close of the seventeenth century Thomas Tryon, educator and dietary reformer, had again stressed the importance of good character in teachers; and it was hardly surprising that when the Society for Promoting Christian Knowledge laid down qualifications for teachers in its charity schools, the main stress was upon piety rather than academic attainment. A teacher was to be:

(1) A member of the Church of England, of a sober life and conversation, and not under the age of twenty-five years.

(2) One that frequents the Holy Communion.

(3) One that hath a good government of himself and his passions.

(4) One of a meek temper and humble behaviour.

(5) One of a good genius for teaching.

(6) One who understands well the grounds and principles of the Christian religion, and is able to give a good account thereof to the minister of the parish, or ordinary, on examination.

7. *The Advice of W. P. to Mr. Samuel Hartlib, for the Advancement of Some Particular Parts of Learning,* 1648.

(7) One who can write a good hand, and who understands the grounds of arithmetic.

(8) One who keeps good order in his family.

(9) One who is approved by the minister of the parish (being a subscriber) before he is presented to be licensed by the ordinary.

The same requirements were called for in a schoolmistress, except for number (7).[8]

De Mandeville's description of teachers as "starving wretches of both sexes that, from a natural antipathy to working,. . .think themselves qualified to become masters and mistresses of charity schools" was probably occasioned by his bitter opposition to educating the poor, and does not represent a fair picture of eighteenth century teachers. Some were undoubtedly lazy, ignorant and ill-equipped both mentally and emotionally for their work; but there were others who left a lasting impression upon the children they taught. C. R. Pemberton, for example, who was at a Unitarian charity school in Birmingham in the seventeen-nineties, said that he owed more to his teacher than he did to any man on earth, except his father. G. J. Holyoake, radical politician, publisher and secularist, wrote in *Sixty Years of an Agitator's Life* of the same teacher with equally affectionate gratitude. Undoubtedly tremendous differences existed between individual teachers, though insufficient evidence exists for a comprehensive account of this subject. There were cases of appalling cruelty on the part of those to whose care children were committed, while others carried out a difficult task to the best of their ability.

In practice, the only valid distinction between charity school teachers and those who taught in private schools was a financial one. There is some reason to believe that

8. See *An Account of the Charity-Schools Lately Erected in Those Parts of Great Britain Called England and Wales*, 7th Ed., 1708, p. 4. See also Asher Tropp, *The School Teachers*, London, 1957, p. 6. There is one recorded instance of an eighteenth century teacher who was a free-thinker. This was Peter Annet, who taught in Liverpool and Lambeth, and who wrote a successful manual of shorthand (which went to three editions) and a number of anti-religious pamphlets. See E. Twynam, *Peter Annet, 1693-1769*, London, ND.

teaching in a school where pupils paid a weekly sum for instruction was a job which could be combined with another calling. There was William Woodcock, schoolmaster and baker, who boasted to William Howitt that he nourished the minds and bodies of his pupils; while James Woodhouse combined the trades of teacher and cobbler at Rowley, two miles from Shenstone's estate, The Leasowes. Such teachers, unlike those in charity schools, had to depend mainly upon the small weekly sums paid to them by their pupils. (Information regarding the fees paid for instruction is not clearly recorded, but from various references in contemporary autobiographies the amount paid for each pupil appears to have varied between one penny and three pence per week.) "I got no more than a penny each week for readers, and three halfpence for writers, so that my wages were small and ill paid", complained David Love in his autobiography. It is, then, hardly surprising that some teachers found it necessary to follow two occupations, or that many others were old women who could earn a few pence in no other way, and by running a rudimentary school were able to eke out a livelihood notable for its poverty.

Charity school teachers, on the other hand, worked full-time for a salary; and the average amount paid to men was about £30 yearly, often with a house and coal, while women received a smaller sum.

The Charity School in Soho, which was founded in 1699 and was still in operation two hundred years later, offers an illuminating and possibly typical example of payments to men and women teachers, with other information regarding pensions and the perquisites which often went with these posts in charity schools. These details are reproduced in Appendix (i). Teachers' saleries were not, however, paid according to a general fixed scale. Henry Hitchcock, for example, who was appointed master of the Aldersgate Ward School in 1748, was paid "the Usual Salary of 20£ p. Annum with all the accustom'd perquisites".

An advertisement for a schoolmaster for the St. Sepulchre, Holborn, Charity School in 1774 read as follows:-

"The office of Schoolmaster for the Boys Charity School of St. Sepulchre's London being vacant by the Resignation of the late Master, any person who wou'd wish to succeed him therin (sic), may send in proper Testimonials of his Character & Abilities to the Treasurer Mr. Jones No. 3 King Street Snowhill on or before the 3ᵈ of Janʳʸ next and attend at a Meeting of the Treasurer and Trustees of the said School to be held at the Schoolhouse in Cocklane on the said 3ᵈ of Janʳʸ next at 4 o'clock in the Afternoon precisely to anwʳ such questions as shall be asked them.

N.B. The Salary is 30£ pʳ Ann. with a House and other Perquisites which may be known by Applying to the Treasurer."

This advertisement and the method of selection were typical of eighteenth century practice, as shown by abundant evidence to be found in the MS records of several charity schools in the City of London, which are preserved in the Guildhall Library. There is, however, a record of an exceptional procedure in the parish of Edmonton, under which the Vicar was appointed schoolmaster on the understanding that he would find a substitute. In 1742 the Rev. Cook was chosen as schoolmaster under all the local educational charities, and he chose James Ware as his usher at £20 per year, with use of the house.[9]

Another unusual practice in the same parish was that of paying the teacher according to the number of children in the school. In 1724 Thomas Hare, then Parish Clerk of Edmonton, was appointed to teach twenty poor boys writing, reading and accounts, for which he was to receive 20s. per annum per boy under a local charity.

Women teachers were generally married, and there was no objection to a husband and wife holding appointments in the same school. It seems evident, especially from the details given of the Soho school, that the turnover of women was very much greater than that of men.

9.   William Robinson, *The History and Antiquities of the Parish of Edmonton*, London, 1819, p. 179. This practice had been specifically forbidden at St. Anne's Charity School, Blackfriars, in 1717. Teachers could only find a substitute if they were sick.

The qualifications laid down by the Society for Promoting Christian Knowledge appear to represent the only attempt during this period to formulate any standards for those offering elementary instruction – and in many cases these must have remained an ideal impossible of realisation both in terms of knowledge and of personality. On the rare occasions when teachers are recalled by their pupils, the resulting picture is generally romanticised and provides little help in arriving at an estimate of the abilities and effectiveness of teachers in eighteenth century elementary schools. "Nor have I forgotten . . .", wrote George Mogridge, "my old schoolmistress, with her spectacles on her nose, sat in the great arm-chair, scolding and hearing lessons."[10]

A serious discussion of the personal attributes required in a teacher is, however, to be found not in a book dealing with educational theory or practice, but in a history of Birmingham which appeared in 1781. Its author was William Hutton, who had been born of poor parents in Derby in 1723. His experiences at school had been far from happy, and he had suffered a good deal at the hands of a particularly brutal schoolmaster. It was probably the memory of this that prompted him to write about teachers at some length, many years later.

Hutton's account of Birmingham Charity Schools is prefaced by some general remarks upon education which stress his view that the personality of the teacher is of supreme importance if children are to be educated, rather than flogged into learning something that they will soon forget. He begins by emphasising the importance of education:

"The direction of youth seems one of the greatest concerns in moral life, and one that is least understood . . . If an ingenious master has flogged the a b c into an innocent child, he thinks himself worthy of praise. A lad is too much terrified to march that path, which is

10. *The Boy's Week-Day Book*, London, 1833. Mogridge, who often wrote as "Old Humphrey", was a prolific author of children's books in the first half of the nineteenth century. He was born in 1787, and his publications all had a strongly evangelical bias. See *Memoir of Old Humphrey*, London, ND (circa 1853).

marked out by the rod. If the way to learning abounds with punishment, he will quickly detest it; if we make his duty a task, we lay a stumbling-block before him that he cannot surmount. We rarely know a tutor to succeed in training up youth, who is a friend to harsh treatment."

Hutton continues by deploring bad relationships between boy and master, quoting Busby, whose name "sounded with horror for half a century after he had laid down the rod". Next, he contrasts what goes on inside a school with the life outside it, and notes the pleasure of boys at breaking-up time, their only care being to forget school.

Looking beyond the classroom, Hutton sees the task of the teacher as primarily to form a member of society:

"If the master thinks he has performed his task when he has taught the boy a few words, he as much mistakes his duty, as he does the road to learning: this is only the first stage of his journey. He has the man to form for society with ten thousand sentiments."

He continues:

"It is curious to enter one of those prisons of science, and observe the children not under the least government: the master without authority, the children without order; the master scolding, the children riotous .... They act in a natural sphere, but he is in opposition: he seems the only person in the school who merits correction; he, unfit to teach, is making them unfit to be taught."

The trouble is, Hutton complains, that many teachers do not consider whether their talents are suited to teaching, but are simply concerned with what profit they can derive from the job. For the others, "the discerning few, who can penetrate the secret windings of the heart; who know that nature may be directed, but can never be invented; that instruction should ever coincide with the temper of the

instructed[11], or we sail against the wind; that it is necessary the pupil should relish both the teacher and the lesson
. . . .", Hutton has nothing but praise. Such teachers, he
considers, are the valuable few who banish tyranny and
introduce in its stead love and reason, so that teacher and
pupil are upon friendly terms, and what is often an irksome
task will be transformed into a rewarding human relationship.

Hutton's views contributed nothing to the eighteenth
century discussion – such as it was – concerning the quality
of popular education. Teachers were rarely mentioned, and
even if these ideas had been published elsewhere than in a
somewhat rambling history of Birmingham, it is extremely
doubtful whether they would have gained any but the
sketchiest currency amongst his contemporaries. Like Paine
with his plan for state-aided education for all, Hutton's
penetrating remarks upon the human qualities required by
teachers evoked no visible response on the part of his
readers. Their interest lies in the fact that they sprang
directly from the author's experience, and were not the
outcome of a theory of education which regarded piety as
the most important quality that a teacher could possess.

However intrinsically interesting this element of
empiricism in Hutton's discussion may be, unfortunately it
adds little to our knowledge of what the eighteenth century
teacher was like as a human being, although his comments
point to the conclusion that many teachers in fact fell
short of the standards he describes. Other evidence available
derives mainly from biographies, autobiographies and
diaries, and the fragmentary nature of some of this material
causes it if not to obscure the subject under investigation,
then to prompt further questions rather than provide
reliable information. In the absence of completely satisfactory records, such material as has survived must be
examined in order to present – in however incomplete a

11. cf. *Raising the School Leaving Age,* Working Paper No. 2, The
Schools Council, London, 1965, p. 3: "It is now well established
that the schools are likely to be most successful with those
pupils whose interests, motivation and sense of relevance are
engaged by the work they are asked to do".

form — a more detailed picture of the eighteenth century elementary school teacher.

These reservations are illustrated by the obscurity which surrounds the life of an extremely successful charity school master, Henry Dixon, who was born in 1675 and died in 1760. Before he was 20, Dixon was master of St. Andrew's School in Holborn, and from here he was recommended in 1711 by Robert Nelson [12] to the charity school in Bath; but whether he spent the remainder of his life there is not known. Dixon was reputed to be a man of great piety, and he also had a great interest in church music, on which subject he wrote a tract. Another of his publications, *The Parents and Schoolmasters Spiritual Assistant for Grounding their Children . . . in Sound Christian Principles, According to the Church of England,* appeared after his death; but his most celebrated book was *The English Instructor.* This was one of the most successful elementary textbooks of the eighteenth century, and its popularity lasted until well into the nineteenth — a 68th edition was published in London in 1822.

Almost contemporary with Henry Dixon was Thomas Dyche, who was educated at the Free School in Ashbourne, Derbyshire. After taking holy orders he moved to London, where he kept a school in Dean Street, Fetter Lane, in 1708. According to the notice in *The Dictionary of National Biography* he was Master of the Free School at Bow in 1710, but this is almost certainly an error, since a permit for him to run a school in the parish of St. Andrew's, Holborn, is dated 1714:

"I permitt Mr. Dyche to keep a School in my Parish
Signed H. Sacheverell D D
Rector of St. Andrew's
Holbourne"

This permit, which is in Sacheverell's hand, is accompanied by a certificate which states that Thomas Dyche — described as a "Clerk" — has given and received the Holy

12. Nelson, one of the founders of the S.P.C.K., was the author of *A Companion to the Festivals and Feasts of the Church of England,* London, 1704, which went through many editions and was still in print in 1888.

Sacrament in the parish church several times in the past year. It probably refers to the school in Dean Street, Fetter Lane.

On the 19th May, 1715, Dyche was unanimously elected by the Company of Drapers, London, as Master of the Free Grammar School at Bow, a Charity School which had been founded by Mrs. Coborn.[13] The formal confirmation of Dyche's appointment is dated the 7th July, 1715, and is still extant:

"I do appoint and nominate Thomas Dyche Clerk & Hannah his wife to be Master & Mistress of Mrs. Coburn's Charity School in Bow, & do require such poor children of Bow as are to be taught by virtue of the said Charity to resort to the Free School in Bow belonging to the Drapers Company where the said Thomas Dyche and his Wife will be ready to teach and instruct them according to the Direction of Mrs. Coburn's Will.

Robert Hardisty"

The practice of having a husband and wife jointly running a charity school was, as already mentioned, not uncommon in the eighteenth century.

Of Dyche's subsequent career little is known. The brief notice in *The Dictionary of National Biography* says that he probably died between 1731 and 1735. His *A New Guide to the English Tongue,* London, 1709, was used in schools until at least 1830, and his *A New General English Dictionary* had reached a 16th Edition in 1777.

From the little we know of them, both Dixon and Dyche appear to have been men who took very seriously the task of educating the young, and to this end they wrote textbooks which had a span of life considerably exceeding that of their authors. The tattered copies which have survived provide a unique and valuable insight into the methods of these early schoolmasters.

John Collier was better known as "Tim Bobbin" the Lancashire poet; by profession, however, he was a school-

13. The Coborn School for Girls — a semi-independant institution — is still in existence in East London.

master, and several biographies of him exist. His poetry
contains much of the Lancashire local and traditional lore
which was current before the Industrial Revolution, and the
dialect in which it is written preserves a good deal of the
slang, and illustrates forms of speech used by the Lancashire peasantry.

Amongst the several biographies of John Collier mentioned above, the most satisfactory one is that of Jesse Lee
entitled *A Memoir of Mr. John Collier.* This was read at a
meeting of the Manchester Literary and Philosophical
Society on the 15th October, 1839, and was afterwards
printed but not, so far as I am aware, ever published. A set
of proof sheets with numerous MS corrections by the
author is in the Manchester Reference Library. An earlier
life of John Collier by his friend and patron, Richard
Townley, is prefixed to *The Miscellaneous Works of Tim
Bobbin, Esq.*", which was published in Salford in 1811.
Interesting from another point of view are the preface and
biographical note by Samuel Bamford, the Radical, which
he wrote for his edition of Tim Bobbin's poetry in 1850.
Bamford had a sense of history, and saw clearly that Collier
had recorded in his verse an authentic picture of a way of
life that had crumbled away with the coming of industrialism.

John Collier was a country schoolmaster. His father, the
Rev. John Collier, was Master of the Free School at
Urmston, and it was near here that his son John was born
in 1708. Of his education nothing is recorded, but when he
was thirteen he was apprenticed to a weaver. After little
more than twelve months his indentures were cancelled:

"... and young as he then was, Tim commenced
itinerant school-master, going about the country from
one village to another in the neighbourhood, teaching
reading, writing and accounts, giving instructions, chiefly
at nights to adults, whose avocations would not permit
of their earlier attendance; so that his time must have
been assiduously employed."

He continued as a wandering schoolmaster until he was
nearly twenty-one, when he became assistant to Mr.

Pearson, minister and schoolmaster at Milnrow, near Rochdale. The salary for running the school was £20 per year, and this sum Pearson shared equally with his young assistant. In addition to this £10, Collier was permitted to augment his income by running a night school on his own account. Soon afterwards Pearson died, and his assistant was appointed to succeed him. He stayed at Milnrow, with a short break in 1751, until his death in 1786. Besides running the school, where he taught "the Art of English, Writing, Arithmetick and other lawful and useful learning", he was also what the local people termed "an edge-lawyer", writing out indentures for apprentices, agreements and wills, and also offering advice upon legal matters. Surprisingly little is known of his activities as a teacher; his biographers have tended to emphasise the literary side of his work, and references to his school at Milnrow are both few and tantalisingly brief, so that he is remembered by posterity for reasons quite unconnected with the fact that he was a schoolmaster.

Little more can be said about Silas Told, who ran a charity school for John Wesley in the Old Foundery. Born in Bristol in 1711, he went to sea at the age of fourteen, and in 1736 he became a schoolmaster at Staplefoot-Tauney in Essex at a salary of fourteen pounds a year. Despite the fact that he was a successful teacher and had "soon raised a considerable school", there was a dispute over the collection of some firewood which led to his dismissal. Told spent several years in London as a clerk, and came into contact with a number of Methodists; and his capabilities and piety apparently impressed John Wesley, who asked him in 1744 to become master, at a salary of 10s. per week, of the charity school at the Old Foundery, where there were about sixty pupils:

> "All the children were to be present at the Foundery every morning at the five o'clock preaching. The school hours were from six in the morning till twelve, and from one to five. No holidays were allowed."[14]

14. G. J. Stevenson, *City Road Chapel London and its Associations,* ND. (1872), p. 41.

With the assistance of an usher and four monitors Told ran the Foundery School for a little more than seven years. His later career as unofficial chaplain to prisoners under sentence of death in Newgate Prison need not concern us here, although it was to this aspect of his career that Wesley referred warmly in his journal after Silas Told's death in 1778. No mention was made there of his teaching activities; but when in 1790 the founder of Methodism edited Told's autobiography, he described him in the Preface as "a man of good understanding, although not much indebted to education".

By a fortunate chance the diaries of two Sussex school-masters of the eighteenth century have survived, and give, each in a very different way, a vivid picture of the country teacher at this period. Thomas Turner was for a short time the village schoolmaster at East Hoathly. Unfortunately, entries in his diary relating to his school are few:

"June 20 (1755). This day being my birthday, I treated my scholars with about five quarts of strong beer . . ."

And eleven months later:

"May 15, 1756. This day I resigned up my school to Francis Elless."

There is also a brief reference to a sum of money owed him for tuition; but the interest of Turner's diary lies not so much in the day by day running of a country school, about which he says nothing, but rather in the revealing portrait of the diarist which emerges from these pages. We see a man of melancholy temperament and restless energy, given to bouts of heavy drinking followed by remorse, and it is abundantly apparent that the life of a teacher could have offered little scope for his capabilities. In fact, he subsequently became a shop-keeper and general dealer. The intimate account of Turner which he himself wrote in this diary provides perhaps the only truly authentic picture we have of the personality of a teacher over two hundred years ago.

The career of Walter Gale, on the other hand, illustrates the bad relations which could exist between the governors of a school and the teacher they had appointed. Gale, a discharged excise man, was appointed to the Free School at Mayfield, Sussex, in 1750. It was stressed to him that he was to pay particular attention to the manners and behaviour of poor children, and his salary was £16 per annum, though this was later increased by £18. A year after his appointment the number of scholars was fixed at twenty-one, one third of whom were taught writing.

Unfortunately a portion of the diary was lost, and in the next entry, for the 25th April, 1758, we learn that Gale's reputation had sunk very low, and one trustee of the school had called him "a drunken, saucy, covetous fellow". Gale, however, continued in his school until 1771, when he was "removed" for neglecting his duties; but in April of the following year he was still a cause of trouble, and the salary due to him was ordered not to be paid until he put the schoolhouse in order. After this, nothing is heard of him; and this schoolmaster of Mayfield, who had augmented his salary by engraving tombstones, painting inn-signs, writing wills and designing ladies' needlework, disappears into history.

The character of ex-Serjeant Roger Lamb[15] stands in sharp contrast to that of Walter Gale. Lamb was born in Dublin in 1756, and at the age of seventeen he enlisted into the 9th Regiment of Foot, later the Royal Welch Fusiliers. Here he served for eleven years, much of this service being in North America. His autobiography says nothing at all about his education, but when he became a soldier he was sufficiently proficient in certain subjects to be singled out from amongst his fellow recruits:-

"I was employed by a serjeant and his wife to teach their son writing and arithmetic .... I also had plenty of writing to do for the various serjeants and corporals, in making out their reports, etc. These employments placed me above that starvation which my unfortunate comrades were compelled to endure."

When he left the Army in 1784 he became a school-master in Dublin; but all that is known of his work at

15. See *Serjeant Lamb of the Nineth* and *Proceed, Serjeant Lamb*, both by Robert Graves, London, 1940 and 1941.

school is a brief reference to him in an anniversary pamphlet:

"For many years the school met in the 'lobby' of the chapel, but in 1791 this house (i.e. the Widow's House in Whitefriar Street) was built. The best known of its teachers was Roger Lamb, who for nearly forty years superintended it with great fidelity to God and great advantage to the boys under his care."[16]

Clearly Lamb was one of the teachers who took his task seriously. Unfortunately, although his autobiography contains a great deal of interesting material, there is nothing relative to his teaching career in Dublin, or even to his own education.

Another schoolmaster, Benjamin Starkey, is somewhat more revealing, and his autobiography, together with the correspondence elicited by it,[17] throw an interesting light upon eighteenth century schools. Born of poor parents in London in 1757, Starkey was taught reading and spelling before he was seven in the school run by his mother. After this he went to a master who taught him to write, and his education was completed at a third establishment. At the age of fourteen he was apprenticed to Mr. Bird, who ran a school in Fetter Lane off Holborn, and in a short while he was running his own school, which he left in the charge of a substitute while he went to Newcastle. Upon his return he found that the number of pupils had dropped from twenty-five to ten, and from his subsequent removal to Sunderland, where he became assistant in a school, we conclude that his private venture had proved unsuccessful. Little more is said about his teaching experiences.

Not long after publication of this autobiography, an article by William Hone based on Starkey's life appeared in *The Every-day book*, and this called forth a letter from Charles Lamb, who was a frequent contributor. His sister

16. Rev. W. B. Lumley, *Methodist Church, Stephen's Green, Dublin. A Jubilee Memorial 1843-1893*, London, ND (1893).

17. *Memoirs of the life of Benj. Starkey...Written by Himself,* Newcastle, 1818. See also W. Hone (Ed.), *The Every-Day Book,* Vol. 1, London, 1826, p.461 ff.,pp. 483-485, pp. 755-756.

had been a pupil of Starkey's — who, however, had left Mr.
Bird's school about a year before her brother too became a
pupil there — and Starkey was remembered with affection;
but Lamb's recollections of Mr. Bird's school are more
sober than Starkey's earlier description of its founder as
"an eminent writer and teacher of languages and mathe-
matics" appear to suggest.

> "It was in fact a humble day-school, at which reading
> and writing were taught to us boys in the morning, and
> the same slender erudition was communicated to the
> girls, our sisters, etc., in the evening."

The school-room itself was in the passage which led from
Fetter Lane to Bartlett's Buildings, and overlooked a dingy
garden. "I remember", continued Lamb, "our legs wedged
in to those uncomfortable sloping desks, where we sat
elbowing each other." According to Mary Lamb, Starkey
had trouble in controlling the girls, and on one occasion —
he was at this time only fourteen or fifteen — he ran away
from the school and was brought back by his father.

Of the later career of Starkey — who came to be called
"Captain Starkey", though nobody knows why — little is
known. Another of Hone's correspondents, "W.G.T.",
writes with some affection of the drunken old man in
Newcastle who was a local "character", but apparently no
longer connected with the teaching profession.

The career of Joseph Pearson was very different from
that of "Captain" Starkey. Pearson was a Methodist schoolmaster of rigorously evangelical views. He was born in 1774
at Arnold, near Nottingham, and at the age of twelve he
was attending a Methodist Sunday School in St. Michael's
Lane, Derby. In the absence of the regular teacher Pearson
took his place, and was so successful that in 1796 he
became Superintendent of the Methodist Sunday School in
Nottingham, when the number of boys had increased to
two hundred. Pearson felt that his task, both here and in
teaching generally, involved something more than simply
instruction, and he carried out much welfare work amongst
the boys at his school. This took the practical form of
supplying them with shoes and stockings. He was in no

doubt, moreover, concerning the aims of instruction in reading, and held that the teaching which his boys received at school should be followed up with religious tracts:

> " ... He wished their minds to be fed with useful knowledge, and he adopted this course (i.e. the distribution of religious tracts) as the cheapest and easiest medium of effecting his wishes."[18]

Little seems to have been recorded of women teachers. Charles Lamb recalled one of them whose school he had attended from about 1779 to 1781:

> "And prim Betsy Chambers,
> Decayed in her members,
> No longer remembers
> 　　Things as she once did."[19]

Thomas Hood, the poet, described her as "an elderly lady, formal, and flaxen-wigged, looking remarkably like a flaxen-haired doll"; but the teacher under whom Charles Lamb first learned to read remains a shadowy figure.

Mary Fletcher, née Bosanquet, was a contemporary of John Wesley, and at one time ran a boarding school for destitute children at Leytonstone. Her school was run on strict Methodist lines,[20] and her description of the daily routine provides a chilling example of how Wesley's educational theories could work out in practice. In a pamphlet published anonymously in 1764, entitled *A Letter to the Rev. Mr. John Wesley*, she is quite explicit about the way her school is run:

> "Our Method of educating our Children is this. As our Design is to fit them for good Servants, we endeavour as early as possible to inure them to Labour, Early Rising and Cleanliness. We have eleven. Three of these (two of

18. H. Fish, *Memoirs of Joseph Pearson*, 1849.
19. Quoted by R. L. Hine, *Charles Lamb and his Hertfordshire*, London, 1949, p. 254.
20. For details of her life see L. F. Church, *The Early Methodist People*, London, 1948, and *More about Early Methodist People*, London, 1949. For Wesley's view of education, see A. H. Body, *John Wesley and Education*, London, 1936.

whom are eleven years old, the other between nine and ten) rise at four. One lights the Nursery Fire, one mine, the other, that below. At five the rest of the Family are called . . . ."

The school day was a long one: prayers at half past six followed by breakfast at seven. Lessons lasted from eight to twelve, and lunch was at one. Except on Saturdays, lessons began again at two and lasted until five; supper was at six, a wash at half past, and bed at seven. As a special concession the little ones were allowed to run in the garden for a quarter of an hour, but, said Mary Fletcher, "they do so with a degree of seriousness; and they know it is for their Health". She continues:

" . . . . We never use the Term Play, nor suffer any to give them those Toys or Playthings, which Children are usually brought up to spend half their time in."

The effects which this bleak regime must have had upon the children can hardly be imagined. Fortunately, not all schools were run upon these unusually Spartan lines. As early as 1711 one teacher, John Honeycoat, had been in trouble because his boys in the charity school at Clerkenwell had performed "Timon of Athens" before an invited audience, and the Bishop of London was petitioned to withdraw his licence. Whether he did so or not is unknown, but it is probable that the licence was not withdrawn, for Honeycoat later became Parish Clerk of Clerkenwell, and contributed to *New Remarks of London by the Company of Parish Clerks,* London, 1732; and at one time Schoolhouse Yard in the same parish was known as Honeycoat Yard.

From this survey of eighteenth century teachers it is possible to draw several conclusions. There was no method of training teachers, and anybody who wished to do so could open a private-venture school. While it was possible to combine teaching with another occupation, masters and mistresses appointed to charity schools under the auspices of the Society for Promoting Christian Knowledge were full-time teachers who were chosen after interview by a committee. It was possible to become a teacher at an early age, and if Benjamin Starkey's apprenticeship is in any way typical of eighteenth century practice, it provides an interesting anticipation of the monitorial system and the pupil-teacher scheme of training which succeeded it.

An unidentified cutting from an eighteenth century newspaper in D. Lysons' *Collectanea,* Vol. 1, speaks of ". . . School-Masters as are going from House to House a begging Children". This indicates clearly the low standing of those who taught reading and writing – and probably the absence of any kind of training would explain it. It does seem clear, however, that in fact there were more teachers who were able to impart at least the elements of reading than this lack of training would suggest.

## II PUPILS

Information regarding the way in which pupils saw their education can be gleaned from a number of auto-biographies some of which were extremely forthright.

" . . . I now", wrote William Hutton, "went to school to Mr. Thomas Meat, of harsh memory, who often took occasion to beat my head against the wall, holding it by the hair, but never could beat any learning into it: I hated all books but those of pictures."

Fortunately, not all those men of humble origins who wrote later in life about their eighteenth century school-days dwelt upon such painful experiences as Hutton's. He became a successful bookseller and author, and while we may regret that in the course of a long and interesting autobiography he says so little about his education, the omission is scarcely irreparable, for a number of "self-made men" have provided accounts of their school days which are characterised by a refreshing candour and a lack of that affectation and tendency to moralise which their changed assumptions and attitudes, resulting from wealth, fame or even notoriety, might lead one to expect.

Before turning, however, to autobiography, it is worth while looking at one of the earliest biographies of a working man to be written and published in England. Not only does it show clearly the difficulties which attended the development of personal education once the brief period of schooling was passed, but the life of the subject illustrates the tragic tension that could occur in the transition to a "higher station" in life.

Stephen Duck, born in Wiltshire early in the eighteenth century, worked as a thresher. His very slight poetic talent, and the publication of a book of verse, caused him to be taken up by society in London, and eventually he became a clergyman. His life ended tragically when he drowned himself. A biography of him,[21] although written in a faintly patronising tone, provides a clear indication of the fact that as a labourer's son he was taught to read, and that he possessed an unusual determination:

" . . . 'tis necessary in the first place to let you know that my friend Stephen, had originally no other Teaching than what enabled him to read and write English, nor that any otherwise than at a Charity School. He has never taken a Single Step towards any other Language, Arithmetick, you know, is generally joined with this degree of learning."

After leaving school at about the age of fourteen, he worked as a day-labourer with his father; the hours were so long that "he could get a little time, which was chiefly o' Nights to read in". It was at this time that he made friends with a man who had been in service in London for two or three years, and who had returned to the country with a small collection of books which he had evidently chosen with care:

" . . . He had learn'd a little which were good Books to read. He had purchased some, and Stephen had always the use of his little Library; which by this time possibly may be encreas'd to two or three Dozen of Books. This Friend knew no more art of English than Stephen; but by talking together they mutually improv'd each other."

Together the two friends read the Bible, Milton, "The Spectator", Addison in defence of Christianity, and other learned works, including translations from Greek, all of which they were able to manage because "they had an English Dictionary and a sort of an English Grammar".

21. J. Spence, *A Full and Authentick Account of Stephen Duck, the Wiltshire poet*, 1731.

Such was the basis of Stephen Duck's education – learning to read at a charity school, working as a labourer and reading at night. To read after a day's work meant coping not only with bodily fatigue, but also with the problem of artificial light, which would have been primitive enough in a labourer's cottage. At times, indeed, he carried a book to work with him, and by working harder than anybody else he was able to snatch half an hour's reading time "without injuring his Master".

In considering eighteenth century autobiographies which describe experience of elementary education against humble backgrounds, a query naturally arises as to how typical of their time the writers of these autobiographies were. Clearly the answer must be that men like Thomas Holcroft, James Lackington, Francis Place, William Hone, Richard Carlile, John Clare and others, were exceptional in that they struggled from difficult circumstances and, in their own lifetimes at least, made a name for themselves – indeed, in several cases their reputation has been enduring. We can, however, judge from their writings that the educational experiences which they describe were shared with their less articulate contemporaries, and thus the autobiographies we are about to examine provide an invaluable view of the poor child at school in the eighteenth century - and while it is impossible to be precise about the number of poor children who attended school it must, if we are to judge from the number of charity schools alone, have been substantial.

An early autobiographical account of elementary education occurs in the *Memoirs of Thomas Holcroft*, the novelist and playwright. Holcroft's description of his early life is of particular interest for the remarkably unsentimental picture it gives of his family circumstances and the near poverty into which the unfortunate father dragged his family. "I was born", he wrote, "in London, in Orange Court, Leicester Fields, on the 10th day of December, 1745, old style." When he was very young he cried to go to school, and an apprentice – Holcroft senior at this time had a shoemaker's shop – was ordered to take the child to a school in the neighbourhood, "where children were sent

rather to keep them out of the way, than to learn anything".

Shortly after this, when Holcroft was about six, there
came a distressing change in his father's fortunes, and the
family moved from London to a remote corner of
Berkshire. It was here that his father taught the boy to
read.

" ... The task at first I found difficult, till the idea one
day suddenly seized me of catching all the sounds I had
been taught from the arrangement of the letters; and my
joy at this amazing discovery was so great, that the
recollection of it has never been effaced. After that my
progress was so rapid that it astonished my father."

Very soon the boy was reading well, and had to read
eleven chapters a day of the Old Testament to his father. A
gift of two chapbooks from the apprentice already mentioned, who used to visit the family, was recalled with
gratitude:

" ... One was the History of Parismus and Parismenes,
and the other, of the Seven Champions of Christendom.
These were to me an inestimable treasure that often
brought the rugged, good natured Dick to my remem-
brance, with no slight sense of obligation."

Elsewhere Holcroft says that these little books were "soon
as familiar to me as my catechism, or the daily prayers I
repeated kneeling before my father. Oh, how I loved poor
Dick!".

Although Holcroft speaks of his vague memory of being
at school — "I have a faint notion of having been among
boys with their school-books" — it is clear that he gained
little from such attendance. Fortunately his father was able
to teach him to read, and the gift of chapbooks provided
an opportunity to delight in his new-found skill. In a later
chapter the nature of such "chapbooks" will be examined,
together with the part they played in the lives of the poor
of the eighteenth century, in just such a way as Thomas
Holcroft described.

An air of almost jaunty confidence characterises James Lackington's account in his Memoirs of his education at a dame school at Wellington, Somerset, where he was born in 1746:

" . . . As I was the eldest, and my father for the first few years a careful hard-working man, I fared something better than my brothers and sisters. I was put for two or three years to a day school kept by an old woman; and well remember how proud I used to be to see several ancient dames lift up their heads and eyes with astonishment, while I repeated by memory several chapters out of the New Testament, concluding me from this specimen to be a prodigy of science. But my career of learning was soon at an end, as my Mother became so poor that she could not afford the mighty sum of twopence per week for my schooling."

Two points in this account call for comment. First, we can infer from what follows in the autobiography that Lackington was able to read when he left the school. Secondly, the amount paid to the teacher at a dame school or similar "private" establishment seems to have varied. For example, another poor boy, Samuel Drew, went to a school in St. Austell, Cornwall, where reading only was taught at one penny per week. On the other hand, a garrison school in Gibraltar in the seventeen fifties charged one penny per week for "schooling", and this was later raised to one penny half-penny per week, while C. R. Pemberton's mother paid 3d. per week for his education at a dame school in the last decade of the century.

In later life Lackington became an extremely successful bookseller and pioneer of cheap books. The exterior of his establishment, known in his own day as "The Temple of the Muses", is still to be seen in the City of London. His earliest recorded venture in bookselling was undertaken when he was little more than twelve, when he sold almanacs at Christmas, undercutting the normal prices charged by the pedlars or chapmen who used to sell these ephemeral publications along with chapbooks.

William Gifford, first editor of the "Quarterly Review", was born in 1756. His father was unstable, and after his marriage ran away to sea, leaving his wife with scanty resources to bring up the boy. These amounted to little more than the rent of two or three small fields:

" ... With these, however, she did what she could for me; and as soon as I was old enough to be trusted out of her sight, sent me to a schoolmistress of the name of Parret, from whom I learned in due time to read. I cannot boast much of my acquisitions at this school; they consisted merely of the contents of the 'Child's Spelling Book'; but from my mother, who had stored up the literature of a country town which, about half a century ago, amounted to little more than was disseminated by itinerant ballad-singers, or rather, readers, I had acquired much curious knowledge of Catskin, and the Golden Bull, and the Bloody Gardener, and many other histories equally instructive and amusing".

["The Golden Bull" and "The Bloody Gardener's Garland" were both popular chapbooks; and again it is interesting to note the part that these played in his early education].

At the age of eight Gifford was sent to the free school, where he stayed for three years making, as he said, "a most wretched progress". Later, a patron was instrumental in helping the boy to improve his knowledge of writing and English Grammar, so that he could go to Oxford. Gifford's subsequent career as a writer and actor certainly justified the help he had been given. A note in his 1816 edition of Johnson's *Works* suggests that the memory of the chapbooks he read in childhood remained in his mind; and in a note on "Westminster Meg" (i.e. Long Meg of Westminster) whose adventures were long popular in chapbook form, Gifford remarks that she performed many wonderful exploits about the time that Jack the Giant-Killer flourished.

In his manuscript autobiography, Francis Place has a great deal to say about his education, the account of the schools he attended being a unique record of how a poor boy was educated towards the end of the century. Place,

who was born in 1771,[22] first went to a school in Wine
Office Court, London, when he was seven or eight. His
father, a journeyman and later a master baker, could sign
his name, so his son tells us, but could not write a business
letter and had probably never read a book in his life. Place
and his brother, however, were sent to be educated:

" . . . The school was kept by a tall stout well looking
man named Jones, proverbially 'savage Jones'. This name
he got from the boys of his own school and from those
of two other schools in the neighbourhood in consequence of the frequent punishment he inflicted on the
boys and the delight he seemed to take in punishing
them. There were about 120 boys in this school. There
were two very large rooms each occupying the whole side
of the house excepting the narrow staircases, one on the
first and the other on the second floor, both of which were
used as school rooms. The doors of these rooms were in the
middle and opened immediately onto the staircases, from
the doors to the opposite sides of the rooms were passages
formed by the ends of the desks which were perpendicular
to the passages. The master sat at a desk at the right of the
room, the usher at the left hand, and they had a perfect
view of the whole of the boys. In this school the boys were
taught to read and write and some to cipher as it was called.
The spelling book was Dilworths[23], the reading book the
Bible. The only book I ever saw in the school for teaching
Arithmetic was Dilworths School Masters Assistant. School
hours were from 9 to 12 and from 2 to 5. The mode of
teaching was this. Each of the boys had a column or half a
column of spelling to learn by heart every morning. He also
wrote a copy every morning. In the afternoon he read in
the Bible and did a sum, on Thursdays and Saturdays he
was catechised, that is he was examined in the Church of
England Catechism, for which an hour was alloted from 12

22. The standard biography is Graham Wallas, *The Life of Francis
    Place*, London, 1898 (Revised Ed., 1918). Quotations used in
    this account of Place's education are from the MS autobiography.
23. Almost certainly this was a *New Guide to the English Tongue,* a
    very popular textbook which was used, in various editions, from
    at least 1751 to about 1836.

till 1 and the afternoons were holidays. The master on the side of the school and the usher on the other side called six boys in rotation out of the forms, who passed the master or usher and stood in a row at the end of the desk, the boy nearest to the master read his lesson or spelled his column or showed his sum and was dismissed to his seat, if any one failed he was obliged to go out and stand at a short distance from the master holding out first one hand and then the other to receive on each a stroke with a stout cane, the strokes were from two to twelve in extreme cases fourteen have been given. This punishment was very severe, and was more or less so as the master was in a good or bad humour. A few strokes would swell the hand considerably and when they intended would bruise the hand sadly. If a boy endeavoured to evade the blow or shrunk from it, he was sure to have a rap on the other side to make him hold his hand fair, and such was the dexterity of the master that he could spread the blows all over the hand, and when he meant to be more severe than usual he would make the end of the cane reach to the wrist. The usher was not allowed to beat the boys, but was obliged to send them to the master with a mark on their book or slate denoting the number of blows they were to have. In the lower room there were two ushers, they had the care of the smaller boys and treated and taught them or neglected them as they pleased. If any person made complaint of the treatment of their boys, the answer was, that the rules of the school could not be broken. If any one complained of anything which occurred in the court after the boys left the school, the reply was, the master had nothing to do with the boys out of school."

Francis Place was at this school until he was nearly twelve, and he tells us that punishment was a constant topic of conversation, and that the boys vied with each other to see how many strokes they could take without wincing.

He next went to a school in Windsor Court, near the New Church in the Strand, where there were never more than forty boys, and seldom as many. The regime here was not as it had been in his previous school:

" . . . There was a head boy and a weekly monitor, each of the boys in the first form being monitors in turn. The head boy heard all the boys on his side of the school and on the cross bench read, each once every other day, spell on the other days, and he had to examine their sums every day. If he thought proper he sent the boy he had heard to the master and if the master found him deficient he punished him. The monitor had reference to the head boy as the head boy had to the master, thus every boy in the first class was examined twice and every boy in the second class three times before he was punished. The system was a mild one, and the punishments were a double task, remaining in the school room for an hour, or for the whole of the dinner time, or a few slaps on the hand were given with a leather strap. The master, a Mr. Bovis was a good man, greatly beloved by his pupils."

Place, who eventually became head boy of the school, went on to speak in very warm terms of Mr. Bovis, and the excellent relationship that he maintained with his pupils. Despite this, Place felt in general that the education he had received was very bad, particularly when compared with that of the nineteenth century.

" . . . The education which I have described was the education which at the time the children of common London tradesmen generally received. Generally it seldom exceeded Reading, Writing and common Arithmetic, badly taught, to this however must be added the Lords Prayer and the Catechism by rote everything else was omitted."

I have quoted at some length from Francis Place's autobiography because it contains details of the running of two eighteenth century schools that are not to be found elsewhere. As an educational reformer Place has received something less than his due, and the vividness with which he recreates the scenes of his early schooling makes it hard to resist the impression that these were significantly formative experiences which helped to shape his thought and activity in the field of education at the beginning of the nineteenth century.

The antiquary, John Britton, was born in rural Wiltshire in the same year as Francis Place. There is a sharp contrast between their early lives — both were born of poor parents, but there the similarity ends. Britton's country upbringing was notable for what he called the "drowsy monotony" of his village where, he says:

" ... I do not think there was a newspaper or magazine purchased by one of the inhabitants before the year 1780, when the London riots were talked about and wondered at."

Village life was enlivened by periodical visits from a clothier, and less frequently a mountebank. A greater contrast with London could hardly be imagined, and there is no reason to suspect that the picture he gives was in any way untypical of the more remote rural scene in eighteenth century England. Even here, however, it was possible for a poor boy to be taught his letters at a dame school:

" ... I learnt the 'Chris-cross-row' from a hornbook, on which were the alphabet in large and small letters, and the nine figures in Roman and Arabic numerals."

Britton's father was a maltster, baker, shop-keeper and small farmer; but for various reasons the family fortunes deteriorated, and after attending several other schools John Britton was apprenticed to a wine merchant in London. The early chapters of his autobiography provide an authentic glimpse of life in an eighteenth century village; and from these beginnings Britton eventually became a distinguished antiquary.

The hornbook which he mentions was not simply a quaint survival in the countryside. William Hone, who was born in 1780, recalled its use in the dame school he attended before he was six years old. Hone, son of a solicitor's clerk, was taught to read by his parents, who used the Bible as a textbook, so that when he was sent to Dame Bettridge — the family was increasing, and he was too young for a boys' school — it was not long before he became her head scholar:

" ... She was very fond of me, and I was always good with her, although, perhaps, naughty enough at home. She lived in one room, a large underground kitchen; we went down a flight of steps to it. Her bed was always neatly turned up in one corner. There was a large kitchen grate, and in cold weather there was always a good fire in it, by which she sat in a carved wooden arm-chair, with a small round table before her, on which lay a large Bible, open, on one side, and on the other a birch rod.

Of the Bible she made great use, of the rod very little, but with fear we always looked upon it. There, on low benches, books in hand, sat her little scholars."

When he was seven, Hone was sent to a boys' day school kept by a Mr. Perry:

" ... The scholars were numerous and well taught for beginners, but my situation was amongst the advanced scholars, who were arranged on forms and at desks. Mr. Perry was a kind, religious man, loving and preserving order, and the scholars were exercised three times a day."

Hone's experiences at school were happy, and it is greatly to be regretted that he wrote so little about Mr. Perry's school.

So far all the autobiographies mentioned have been written by men who achieved some reputation in their lives; but perhaps the most moving narrative of all is the life story written in verse by the blind ex-soldier, James Downing, who lost his sight when serving in Egypt, and wrote an account of his adventures when he returned to England and was discharged from the Army. Born in Truro in 1781, Downing apparently settled in Bedford, and his verse narrative is not without interest. The following three verses are representative of the whole work:

"In Truro, Cornwall, I was born;
But soon my mother died;
Thus by death from me was torn,
And I had lost my guide.

> Thus being left in infancy,
> My father labour'd hard;
> From any thing which he saw good,
> I never was debarr'd.

> "He sent me to a neighbouring School,
> Where I was taught to read;
> But as in stature I advanc'd,
> In sin I did proceed."

Downing's autobiography affords a glance — and it is no more than this — into the life of a private soldier. It demonstrates once more that the elements of education were readily available even to poor children.

A more indirect piece of evidence for this assertion is to be found in the life of Corporal William Todd, a Yorkshireman born in 1725, who kept a journal of his adventures in the Seven Years War. Clearly he had learned to read and to write — but where? At his death he was described as a labourer, yet he was sufficiently well educated to have been employed as a regimental schoolmaster in 1754, and he was by no means the only soldier in the ranks who was able to read and write.

The early life of Joseph Blacket, who became a cobbler, demonstrates again the way in which a poor boy could be educated. He was born in 1786 near Catterick in Yorkshire:

> " ... My father was a day labourer ... I was the youngest, except one, of twelve children, eight of whom were living at the time that I was first sent to school, which was early in youth, owing to the village schoolmistress being very partial to me, and giving me a free education. With her I staid until the age of seven; when another school being opened by a man, whom my parents thought better able to instruct, I was placed by them under his tuition, and continued to write and learn arithmetic till the age of eleven ... "

Blacket was also a minor poet, but his verses — which prompted a malicious epitaph from Byron[24] — will scarcely

24. "But spare him, ye Critics, his follies are past,
   For the Cobbler is come, as he ought, to his *last*".
   Quoted by T. J. Pettigrew, *Chronicles of the Tombs*, London, 1902.

bear a revival. Neither, for that matter, will those of George
Mogridge, the author of numerous evangelically inspired
books for children, many of which were written under the
pseudonym of 'Old Humphrey'. But in one of his heavy-
footed verses Mogridge recalls the chapbooks which he read
as a child:

"And did the magic of romantic lays
Seduce the leisure of my earlier days?
Have idle fictions o'er my fancy stole
And superstition's tale beguiled my soul?"

Born in 1787 at Ashted, near Birmingham, Mogridge
attended a village school. His father was a canal agent, and
so he cannot fairly be described as poor; but his anonymous biographer does comment upon his fondness for the
ballads and chapbooks which he read when he was still a
boy.

In his autobiography Samuel Bamford, the Radical, has a
good deal to say about his education. His father was a
weaver who was not only able to read, but was keenly
interested in books. Samuel Bamford was born near
Manchester in 1788, and it was from his father that the
boy had his first lessons:

" . . . Then in schooling I learned the alphabet from my
father at his loom; I afterwards went a short time to the
parish clerk at the Free School, but I learned not anything there; I was not at that age, quick at imbibing
instruction. On Sundays I went with the bigger children
to the chapel school, which was next door to our house,
until another one was built on the road to Boar-
shaw — but neither did I profit by my Sunday tuition."

Subsequently he went to a local school where he learned
nothing, but comments upon the corporal punishment to
which he was subjected; and then to a Methodist preacher,
where he learned to read words of one syllable. It was not
until he went to the Free Grammar School that he learned
to read well. At first he read nothing but the Bible: "The
New Testament was now my story book", he wrote. But
soon he discovered in Manchester a shop where chapbooks

were sold, and the range of his reading was greatly extended:

> " ... At the corner of Hanging Bridge, near the Old
> Church yard, was a book-shop kept by one Swindells, a
> printer. In the spacious windows of this shop, which is
> now 'The Wedding-Ring Coffee House', were exhibited
> numerous songs, ballads, tales and other publications, with
> horrid and awful-looking woodcuts at their head; which
> publications with their cuts had a strong command on my
> attention. Every farthing I could scrape together, was now
> spent in purchasing 'Histories of Jack the Giant Killer',
> 'Saint George and the Dragon', 'Tom Hickathrift', 'Jack
> and the Bean Stalk', 'History of the Seven Champions',
> tale of 'Fair Rosamond', 'History of Friar Bacon',
> 'Account of the Lancashire Witches', 'The Witches of the
> Woodlands', and such like romances."

Bamford senior characterised these books as trash; but his
son, as we have seen, recalled their titles with affection
long after he had outgrown them.

There are further examples of poor boys learning to
read. Robert Millhouse, for example, was born in Nottingham in 1788 in extreme poverty, and he was sent to work
at the age of six. He was taught to read at a Sunday
School, and later achieved a modest reputation as a minor
poet.

C. R. Pemberton, born in Pontypool in 1790, went to a
dame school, and later to the Unitarian Charity School in
Birmingham. He spent some years as a pressed sailor, afterwards becoming an actor, writer and lecturer, and he was
well known in radical circles until his death in 1840.

Richard Carlile, the radical printer, was born at Ashburton, Devonshire, in 1790. Despite the fact that his
father died before he was five, leaving his mother penniless,
he was sent to school:

> "My first schoolmistress was old Cherry Chalk, who
> taught the alphabet on a horn book ... I had two other
> schoolmistresses of a more respectable stamp than old
> Cherry. I believe the first taught for three-halfpence a
> week, and the other two (sic) at twopence."

A small book published anonymously by Charles Knight in 1845 entitled *Memoirs of a Working Man*, and never subsequently reprinted, contains the life story of a tailor, Thomas Carter. He was born in 1792, and when his father joined the Army two years later, his mother was left to bring up the child on her own. Carter learned to read at home, using the Bible as a textbook — a method which he later criticised:

" ... As a general rule, I think it may be fairly determined that the requiring children or youths to read a given portion of the Sacred Scriptures, at a prescribed time, as a lesson or text, is very injudicious."

When he was still very young Carter made the acquaintance of an old woman who sold cakes, sweets, fruit and chapbooks. He was allowed to read all the chapbooks she had on sale, and he remembered them with pleasure when he came to write his autobiography. He thought very much less of religious tracts than he did of chapbooks:

" ... It did not in those days seem to be understood that abstract treatises on religious or other serious subjects were not adapted to fix the attention of children and other young persons. There was but little recognition of the fact that the human mind needs recreation as well as instruction ... I have now — after an interval of more than forty-five years — a clear recollection of the little books I read when a child, and which then formed part of the poor child's 'Entertaining Library'."

He goes on to talk about the prices of these books, some of which sold for a farthing each, and justifies his discussion of this topic in the following words:

" ... It may seem to be little better than trifling to write about farthing or halfpenny histories of 'Tom Thumb', 'Jack the Giant-Killer', 'Little Red Riding-Hood', and the like; but when it is considered that the human mind generally retains, in mature years, much of the tastes and habits it acquired in childhood, it will not be difficult to believe that important consequences may and often do arise out of circumstances or practices which in themselves are of little worth or moment."

Thomas Carter had a good deal to say about reading, and in the extracts quoted he provides clear evidence that chapbooks were readily available, and provided for poor children in the eighteenth century the only alternative to reading either religions tracts or the Bible. His obvious passion for books permeates his narrative, and clearly he regarded chapbooks as a means to reading better things. In this he was probably untypical, for the majority of those who learned to read in the eighteenth century no doubt saw popular literature – then as now – as providing an end in itself for exercising the reading skills acquired in elementary schools of different kinds; but as history was inevitably to show, the availability of this popular literature proved, by the turn of the century, to have been for many others of its readers the means to a wider taste and range in reading.

Carter's comment upon the use of the Bible as a text-book is echoed by John Clare, the poet, who was born at Helpstone, Northamptonshire, in 1793:

". . . I think the method of learning children in village schools verry (sic) erroneous; that is as soon as they learn their letters, to task them with lessons from the bible, and testament, and keep them digging at them without any change till they leave it."[2][5]

Clare's own schooling was irregular. When his mother had the money he was sent to the village school kept by an old woman, and afterwards to a master who kept a school outside the village; but inability to pay the fees regularly meant that there was no continuity in such instruction as he received. He was therefore forced to supplement his meagre teaching as best he could, and when he worked he saved to buy chapbooks when hawkers offered them for sale at the door and from stalls at fairs and markets. Amongst the books he read were 'Robin

25. E. Blunden (Ed.), *Sketches in the Life of John Clare by Himself,* London, 1931. See also F. W. Martin, *The Life of John Clare,* 2nd Ed., London 1964; and *Clare Selected Poems and Prose,* Ed. E. Robinson and G. Summerfield, Oxford, 1966.

Hood's Garland', 'Joe Miller's Jests', 'Cinderella', 'Jack and
the Beanstalk', and others. All these were popular chapbooks, and from them Clare proceeded to writers like
Defoe and Bunyan — and on one occasion he went to
Stamford, where he purchased Thomson's 'Seasons' for one
shilling and sixpence.

Two further views of education must suffice to complete
this account of how the poor learned to read. James
Watson, the Chartist publisher, was born at Malton in
Yorkshire in 1799, and his father died two weeks after his
birth leaving the widow to bring up the boy and his sister.
Since she was a teacher at one of the Sunday Schools in
the town, she was able to teach her son to read, so that
before he was twelve, as Watson says:

" . . . I could read well, write indifferently, and had a
very imperfect knowledge of arithmetic."

Watson, then, had no formal schooling, unlike William
Lovett, the Chartist, who was born in Newlyn, Cornwall, in
1800, and was in his own words "sent to all the dame-
schools of the town before I could master the alphabet."
Eventually he was taught to read by his great grandmother,
who was then eighty years of age. His recollections of
school were not altogether happy ones:

" . . . Of my first school I remember being sent home at
midsummer with a slip of paper round my hat with my
name on it in red ink, given as a holiday present. Of my
second school was the being put in the coal-cellar for
bad conduct on the second and last day of my being
there."

This somewhat unusual picture of a future radical politician must serve as the final extract here from the evidence
left to us by men of humble origins who acquired some
measure of learning in the eighteenth century. There is no
reason to suppose that the experiences described are
untypical in any other way than the articulateness with
which they were recalled. What, then, can be concluded
from these personal accounts?

One interesting feature of several of them is the revelation that the mother either taught her child to read or saw that he was sent to school. Clare's mother, for example, although illiterate herself, sent him to school whenever she could. The influence of the mother in poor families seems to have been important, and for various reasons she may, in many cases, have supplied the impulse towards achieving a modification of the ignorance which might so easily have been the lot of labouring men and women in Augustan England.

From all these autobiographies it is clear that children from even the poorest homes could have the opportunity – assuming, of course, willingness on the part of their parents – of being taught at least to read. Few of these accounts indicate that the instruction went beyond reading to writing, and fewer still that it extended to the realms of arithmetic. As most of them show, the scope offered for exercising any skill which they acquired in reading was limited by their instructors almost exclusively to the Bible or – as Thomas Carter described them – "abstract treatises on religious or other serious subjects".

In these circumstances, how easy it is to understand the warmth with which Thomas Holcroft, William Gifford, George Mogridge, Samuel Bamford, Thomas Carter and John Clare all recall the part played in their lives by chapbooks. This form of popular literature, which at this time was easily and very cheaply available throughout the kingdom, appears to have fulfilled a need for recreative reading – and a need common to all men and women at all times for giving wing to the imagination.

Before examining this literature more closely, an account of popular education in the eighteenth century must surely look in some detail at the precise implications of the phrase "learning to read".

# Chapter 3

## THE ART OF READING

The most important subject in the limited curriculum of elementary schools in the eighteenth century was reading. In charity schools it was taught, not in order to extend the intellectual powers of poor children, but in order that they might read the Bible and thereby remain content and grateful for their humble role in a society whose system of rigid social stratification had been ordained by God. In those schools where a trifling weekly sum was paid for instruction, reading was the main activity, and there is, as we have seen, some reason to believe that the fee for instruction in it was lower than that for writing.

In any case, it seems reasonable to assume that reading was taught before writing, and the comment of James Rogers, an early Methodist who was born in Yorkshire in 1749, that he "was put to school early and taught to read the Scriptures from a child" simply reflects the pre-eminence of reading as a school subject. As early as 1707 the Rev. James Talbott had written *The Christian School-Master,* a manual for teachers which was popular throughout the eighteenth century, and which stated quite categorically that the teaching of reading – after religious and moral education – was the first task of the teacher, and that writing should only be tackled when children could read "competently well".

It is by no means certain when children went to school, and at what age they learned their letters. In 1701 there appeared anonymously *The Schoolmaster: Being a New Method of Teaching Children, at Three Years Old, to Read and Write English,* the title of which makes a specific suggestion on this point. The anonymous author of *Education of Young Children,* 1742, suggested:

"... when a child can talk, 'tis time he shou'd learn to read. And when he reads put into his hands some easy

pleasant book suited to his capacity wherein the enter-
tainment he finds may draw him on, and reward his
pains in reading."

This recommendation of an "easy pleasant book suited to his
capacity" was not the usual approach during this period; although Crabbe records in his account of a dame school:

"To Learning's second Seats we now proceed,
Where humming Students gilded Primers read;
Or Books with Letters large and Pictures gay,
To make their Reading but a kind of Play -
'Reading made Easy', so the Titles tell;
But they who read must first begin to spell:"

The idea that reading should be taught as soon as
children could speak may have represented eighteenth century practice. Certainly poor children were required to
work at an early age, and opportunities for education were
therefore curtailed, so that they may have had to go to
school at a much earlier age than is now deemed suitable;
and in *Some Particulars of the Life and Experience of
Nicholas Manners* (York, 1785), the writer claimed that "so
diligent was the master that by the time some of us were
six, we could read the Bible ... ". Manners was born in
1732, so that his comment refers to the year 1738. There
seems, however, insufficient evidence for generalising with
any validity about the age at which children started to
learn how to read.

Very much less uncertainty surrounds our knowledge of
the way in which reading was taught. A number of text-
books has survived, and from an examination of them it is
possible to assemble a reasonably accurate picture of
teaching techniques in eighteenth century schools.

Before turning, however, to the question of reading
primers and elementary grammars, it is necessary to consider briefly the means by which generations of children
had learned, and many continued to learn, their
letters — the horn-book. This consisted of a single sheet
upon which was printed the alphabet, the nine digits and
the Lord's Prayer, covered with transparent horn and fixed

in a frame with a handle. According to Andrew W. Tuer[1], the earliest recorded use of a horn-book is about 1450, and they continued to be used in classrooms until about the close of the eighteenth century, though few have survived. Tuer quotes an unpublished note by William Hone, who wrote:

">. . . I remember the horn-book to have been generally used by mistresses of small schools in the metropolis until 1790 or later."

And one correspondent of Andrew Tuer pointed out that the horn-book was "frequently used as an instrument of punishment, and the children had cause to remember a crack upon their craniums administered with the idea of forcing an inlet for the mythical signs that so bothered the juvenile mind".

The decline of the horn-book was probably hastened by the fact that during the eighteenth century books of instruction became both cheaper and more plentiful, and also that a Salisbury printer, Benjamin Collins, hit upon the effective idea of printing the alphabet and the Lord's Prayer upon cardboard which could then be folded, and opened when required for use. Not only were these very much cheaper to produce than horn-books, but they could be sold in large quantities, and would require replacement from time to time.

Battledores, as these cardboard alphabets were called, rapidly became popular, and between 1770 and 1780 Collins claimed that he sold over one hundred thousand of them. They cost him three pounds ten shillings per thousand to print, and he sold them wholesale at twelve shillings per gross. They retailed at twopence each. These early battledores were covered with gilt embossed coloured Dutch paper, and looked extremely attractive — perhaps the first time that it had been thought worth while to make instructional material for children visually appealing. [Battledores were used well into the nineteenth century. One of them in the British Museum collection contains an illustration of the Crystal Palace, and was probably published in 1851.]

1. *The History of the Horn Book*, 2 vols; 1896.

The horn-book and the battledore represented the means by which the alphabet could be taught; and text-books in the eighteenth century carried this instruction a further stage forward by combining letters to make words, due attention being paid to spelling and syllables. The sequence was clearly expressed by James Talbott, who was drawing upon common practice and commending it to the teacher of reading:

> ". . . In order to the First of These (i.e. Reading). after we have gone through the Letters of the Alphabet, we must Instruct them in the true Spelling of Words, and the Distinction of Syllables, by the help of some proper Spelling Book for that Purpose. From this they must proceed to the Reading of Words as they are joined together in a Sentence . . . ."

Even at the beginning of the eighteenth century, the teacher seeking "some proper Spelling Book" had a surprisingly wide choice, and might have selected any one of several primers which were available. If he were traditionally minded, and had only a limited objective in his teaching, "The ABC with the Catechism" would have answered his needs. It consisted generally of the ABC, combinations of letters and the Church catechism; hence it could be used to teach not only the rudiments of reading, but also the essentials of the Protestant religion, and this form of elementary reading book was clearly used as a means of teaching the alphabet. We find, for example, the Trustees of St. Anne's Charity School, Blackfriars, purchasing "20 Testaments with the Catechisms found with them" in 1719; and Alexander Murray, author of the *History of European Languages,* 2 Vols., Edinburgh, 1823 who was born in Scotland in 1775, was taught his letters in this way by his father, a shepherd who bought his son a catechism.

One of its earliest forerunners was *The ABC Set Forthe by the Kynges Majestie and His Clergye,* published in about 1545, which consisted of the alphabet followed by prayers and catechitical instructions. By the reign of Queen Elizabeth the catechism was well established as an educational medium, and in 1626 there was *An ABC or Holy Alphabet.* It continued in use until the close of the eighteenth century, and in the nineteenth its application became very much more widespread – William Pinnock, an educational publisher, issued short catechisms upon eighty-three different subjects, price ninepence each. By the end of the nineteenth century, however, the vogue for catechisms had passed.

An interesting contribution to the technique of using the catechism as an aid to teaching was made by Simon Ford, Rector of Old Swinford, Worcestershire, who published in 1684 *A Plain and Profitable Exposition of and Enlargement Upon the Church Catechism . . . Together With a Shorter Catechism Annexed for the Benefit of the Younger Sort of Catechumens.* The concluding remarks show Ford's awareness of problems in teaching which later developments have shown to be connected with the wider issues of the learning process and the adaptation of material to the child's age and capabilities:

> "The use of these small Questions, is only to make trial, whether the younger Children (not yet of capacity to learn the longer Catechism preceding) do, when they are examined in the Church Catechism, repeat the Answers merely by rote. And if they answer heedlessly, to engage them by reflection upon what they have said, to attend more to the business they have in hand."

The catechism consists mostly of questions in order to "prompt the dullest Child to the Answer he is to make". Clearly Ford is concerned primarily with teaching religion, and there is no ABC with his catechism, but his comments are interesting mainly because of their assumption that dull children require special attention.

In the eighteenth century the potentiality of the catechism was most readily comprehended by Isaac Watts, who saw clearly that this method of instruction would serve both religious and educational ends. His *A Discourse on the Way of Instruction by Catechisms and of the Best Method of Composing Them* had reached a 3rd Edition by 1736, and in it he stresses the fact that children should be instructed in religion, partly by reason and partly by parental authority. Short summaries may be necessary for less able children, and in any case, the best summaries of religion are provided by catechisms, but it is of paramount importance that children should *understand* what they learn by heart. Watts mistrusted a parrot-like repetition, and the catechisms he wrote, which enjoyed a considerable success, show clearly that he had a great deal of sympathy with the young. Elsewhere he expressed clearly his view that reading was the real key to understanding theological matters:

"... But the greatest Blessing that we derive from Reading, is the Knowledge of the Holy Scriptures, wherein God has conveyed down to us the Discoveries of his Wisdom, Power and Grace, through many past Ages; and whereby we attain the Knowledge of Christ, and of the way of Salvation by a Mediator."[2]

Deservedly popular, however, as Watts' catechisms were, many more were issued by the Established Church, and a typical one is *The ABC with the Catechism; that is to say, An Instruction to be Learned of Every Person Before He be Brought to be Confirmed by the Bishop*. [London: printed for the Company of Stationers, 1719]. The verso of the title-page contains a woodcut of a teacher with children, and the numerals are illustrated in both letters and figures, e.g.

| one | seventy |
|-----|---------|
| i | 1xx |
| 1 | 70 |

On page 3 there is the alphabet in both black-letter and Latin type, and from page 4 to the end there is the catechism. Copies of the 1725 and 1750 reprints are preserved in the British Museum, and there were certainly others; but the survival of such ephemeral material, which was in any case subjected to extremely rough treatment by young readers, is a matter of fortunate chance. Quite a number of eighteenth century catechisms are to be found in the British Museum and the Bodleian Library, but they

2. *The Improvement of the Mind,* 2 vols., 1782 (first published 1741).

can represent only a tiny fraction of the numbers which were printed and used.[3]

One of the most interesting developments of the catechism – and one which furthered the thoughts expressed by Simon Ford towards the end of the seventeenth century was its adaptation to the needs of less able children. *The ABC with the Shorter Catechism* was designed "for catechising such as are of weaker capacity". The earliest surviving edition of it that I have been able to trace was published in Edinburgh in 1714, and it was constantly reprinted throughout the century. Further, the general instructions for use of the Church Catechism state that:

". . . The Catechist is at Liberty to vary the Questions, and to ask others according to the Capacity of the Children."[4]

The survival of a catechism published in the middle of the century by the Diceys[5] throws light upon the connection between school books and reading for pleasure. This little book of twenty-four pages is entitled *The A.B.C. with the Shorter Catechism: Appointed by the General Assembly, to be a Directory for Catechising of Such as are of Weak Capacities*. The verso of the title-page consists of a catalogue of eighteen popular chapbook titles printed in Bow Church Yard by the Diceys, and page 3 contains the alphabet, while from page 4 to the end there is a simplified catechism. With its two woodcut illustrations and advertisement for other cheap books, this is not an unattractive little volume, and was clearly intended for use as an elementary reading primer.

3. cf. Cyprian Blagden, *The Distribution of Almanacks in the Second Half of the Seventeenth Century* ("Studies in Bibliography", Vol. XI, Papers of the Bibliographical Society of the University of Virginia, 1958, p. 107 ff): "We are forced to rely for instance on a single mutilated copy of a school book or even on hearsay for our knowledge of a once widely distributed and frequently handled publication".
4. *A New Method of Catechising by way of Question and Answer*, London, 1712, Preface, p. iii.
5. An important and enterprising firm of chapbook printers. See Appendix (ii).

The first stage, then, in learning to read was mastery of the alphabet, and to this end children might use a horn-book or catechism, and later in the century a battledore. Alternatively, a teacher could utilise one of the many elementary text-books which were published, and we must now examine these in order to see *how* children were taught to read. The most striking features of such material are its quantity, and the extent to which popular titles were reprinted.

The earliest English text-books were published in the second half of the sixteenth century, and it is from them that the eighteenth century ones are directly descended. Thomas Newbery's *Booke in Englysh Metre ... Very Pretty for Children to Read ...* appeared in 1563, and in 1569 John Hart published his *Orthographie,* which he followed in 1570 with *A Methode or Comfortable Beginning for all Unlearned whereby They may bee Taught to Reade English in a very short time with pleasure.* This book contained a pictorial alphabet, and "in a great letter the Christian belief, the ten commandments of God, and the Lord's Prayer, where the syllables are sundered for the ease of all learners old and young."[6]

Francis Clement's *Petie Schole with an English Orthography* came out in 1587, and in addition to instruction in reading and writing, covered elementary arithmetic as well as instruction in ink-making and quill cutting. The first part of William Kempe's *Education of Children in Learning* was published in 1588, and like all the books so far mentioned, was thoroughly practical in its approach.

The most popular of these early text-books was Edmund Coote's *The English Schoolmaster,* which was first published in 1596 and had reached a 54th edition in 1737. Quite apart from the thoroughness and practicality of Coote's book — he was master of the grammar school at Bury St. Edmunds — the interesting point about the continuing vogue of *The English Schoolmaster* is the clear indication it

6.    Both of Hart's books are reprinted in B. Daniellson, *John Hart's Works on English Orthography and Pronunciation,* Stockholm, 1955.

offers that the methods of learning to read changed little, if at all, over several centuries. After the alphabet had been learned, letters were combined to form syllables, and syllables were used to make words. There was no serious disagreement about this method in the eighteenth century, and what little discussion there was centred upon the way in which lists of words were presented, and which words were taught. After long lists of words had been spelled and read, children were put to reading simple sentences, usually of a religious nature, and from these they proceeded to more difficult — but equally didactic — passages of English.

An explanation of this procedure is to be found in the instructions which preface John Evans' *The Palace of Profitable Pleasure*, a spelling book which was published in 1621. The author explains his plan:

". . . I thought it necessarie to collect all English words into one small Treatise, that having learned onely this Booke with understanding, they might proceede to the reading either of the holy Scriptures, or of any other Booke, with much facility, for all books doe consist of words."

The aim of his book, Evans goes on, is to enable every one who uses it "to spell and reade every word distinctly, and consequently, every English booke". In order to help the reader, all the words in it are broken into syllables.

Cyprian Kinner's pamphlet *A Continuation of Mr. John-Amos-Comenius*, ND (1648), outlines the way that children should be taught to read English, and stresses that care must be taken in presenting material so that pupils are always proceeding "from the more simple and easie lines, letters and syllables, by the more compounded, to the most compound, and complexed of all". Kinner is explicit about the importance of moving from simple to more difficult material, while for Evans this principle is implicit in the arrangement of his book.

A somewhat different approach to the problem of teaching children to read was suggested by George Snell, whose views on teachers have already been mentioned. He held that the contents of reading books should be simple, and that the method of instruction ought to be closely related to the everyday experience of the pupil:

> "First teach them single names; as father, mother, brother, Daniel, Robert, Peter: sister, Marie, Joan, Lydia ... apple, sugar, nuts, plumbs, bread, flesh, butter, dog, cat, mous ... hand, finger: then bring them to propositional sentences as, the milk is hot; the water is cold; sugar is sweet: thence to reasoning causal; as, this broth will bite your tongue, becaus it hath pepper; I will thank my mother because she gave me this fig: lastly, let him read illative Reason: as, My father is angrie, therefore he will chide: Becaus I have said my lesson well, therefore my mother will love me."

Snell's views evoked no response amongst his contemporaries; nor, with one exception, amongst his successors in the following century. The problem of teaching children how to read was viewed in a very different way.

The fundamental issue was clearly expressed by E. Cole in his *The Young Schollar's Best Companion*, published in 1690, and his statement provides an admirable point of departure for a discussion of the text-books which were used during the eighteenth century:

> "The first thing to be considered by those that would attain to the perfection of Reading well, is perfectly to gain the knowledge of the Characters, or letters that are used, which though in all but Twenty Four in number are different in make and size; and though a Letter is the smallest part of a word, yet from Letters all words are framed; and therefore, it is convenient to let the Beginner see them in their several shapes. . . ."

Cole's book was only one of a group of late seventeenth-century text-books which continued to be used in the early years of the eighteenth. Their bibliography is obscure and their authorship hardly less so; in some cases no copy seems to have survived, and one is forced to rely upon contemporary advertisements[7], or upon Arber's reprint of "The Term Catalogues", for details of them. An examination of those books which have been preserved leads inescapably to the conclusion that they were practical manuals written by men who were engaged in the day to day task of teaching children to read, and their interests lay not in experiment but rather in proceeding in their classroom practice along the well-tried lines that had been laid down by the authors of the earliest English text-books. Among them was Henry Care's *The Tutor to True English*, published in 1687 and reprinted in 1688, 1690 and 1699. In the following year, several primers were published – there was the anonymous *A Key to the Art of Letters, and The Compleat School-Master, or Child's Instructor*, the authors of which were T.T., G.F. and G.C.[8]. There was also John Urmston's *The London Spelling Book*.

Urmston, who is described on the title-page as a "schoolmaster at Kensington", had written what was to be the first of the popular eighteenth century text-books, and although its success was modest enough when compared with that of later writers, it is worth more than a cursory mention. Of Urmston himself nothing is known, and the bibliography of his spelling book is extremely complicated. According to Arber it was first published in 1700, price 6d. There is no copy of this in the British Museum, which possesses only a fourth edition dated 1710. Arber, however, records a twelfth edition "with cuts and amendments" as being announced for publication in 1702. In the absence of surviving copies there is no way of resolving the problem of dates and editions, but the bibliographical confusion, which suggests unauthorised reprintings, does indicate that this was a popular manual.

The Preface to the 4th edition of 1710 is interesting:

7.  See for example "T. W." (Thomas White?), *A Little Book for Little Children*, 12th Ed., London, 1702, which contains advertisements for a number of text-books of which no copy appears to be extant.
8.  T. T. was possibly Thomas Tryon, author of *A New Method of Educating Children*, London, 1695, and of other books.

". . . The great want of Skill in Spelling, not only in the Youth of both Sexes, but even in Persons Adult, hath caused much enquiry after Books of this Sort."

A comment upon contemporary practice that "It is usual to put a Child on, after having Learned the Letters, to spell words of one syllable, and soon to Words of two or three Syllables" leads him to propose that children should first learn words which are familiar to them, regardless of the number of syllables they contain. This idea of relating the teaching of reading to the pupil's experience was not a new one; it had been advanced about fifty years earlier by George Snell. If, however, we are to judge from eighteenth century text-books in which learning by rote was the rule, this method found little favour with the teachers of the period.

The considerable popularity of a book by Thomas White, with its insistence upon memorising lists of words, provides a case in point. The British Museum possesses two copies of his work, *A Little Book for Little Children;* one is a twelfth edition which appeared in 1702, and the other a much shorter, and probably later, version which is undated but contains a frontispiece portrait of Queen Anne. The subject matter in both copies is dull, and there is no attempt to make it interesting or relate it to the child's experience. The earlier edition has an advertisement on the verso of the title-page for other school books which range in price from a spelling book entitled *The School of Vertue* at twopence to Cole's *The Young Schollar's Best Companion,* which cost one shilling, while *Fisher's Spelling Book* cost sixpence.

It is worth noting that the reading matter in Cole's book mentioned above shows a marked anti-Catholic bias, and reflects the attitude of the more extreme supporters of the Protestant Succession. A similar tendency is to be discerned in another text-book of the time, *The Protestant Tutor,* London, 1715, whose anonymous author was as much concerned to combat Catholicism, which he described as "Notorious Errors, Damnable Doctrines . . . of the bloody Papists", as he was to instruct his young readers "in the compleat method of Spelling, Reading and Writing, True

English". Similarly, an anonymous work published in 1704, *The Young Scholar's Best Companion, or a New Spelling-Book from the ABC to the Grammar,* contained a "History of Popish Plots".

Another book which was extremely popular at this time was Tobias Ellis's *The True Royal English School,* which was reprinted in London in 1701. The title-page outlines its scope: "A Catalogue of all the words in the Bible . . . First, beginning with one Syllable and proceeding by degrees to eight, divided and not divided; whereby all Persons of the meanest Abilities, may, with little help, be able to read the Bible over distinctly, easily, and more speedily than in any other method."

The continuing popularity of seventeenth century school books during the earlier decades of the ensuing century is one of the most noteworthy features of the educational scene at this period. Nathaniel Strong, for example, was the author of *England's Perfect Schoolmaster;* a third edition was published in 1681, an eighth in 1699, and a ninth in 1706. An even longer period of popularity was enjoyed by a book written by the Dissenting Minister, Benjamin Keach, called *The Child's Delight: or, Instructions for Children and Youth,* a third edition of which was printed in London in 1703, price 6d., while a thirtieth came out, also in London, in 1763. The title-page of the earlier edition said "Necessary to Establish Young People in God's Truth, in opposition to the Error in these perilous Times", but this had been omitted by 1763, though both books are described upon their title pages as "pleasant and useful". This notion of pleasure before utility is unusual at this period when text-books tended towards a uniform standard of dullness. The contents of Keach's book, however, do not live up to the promise implied, and consist mainly of an ABC with catechism, some reading passages, "A Short Dictionary" and an account of the English coinage. There is an attempt to brighten the subject matter with a series of moralistic verses which are interspersed in the text, and typical of these is "The Good Child's Resolution", of which I quote three verses:

"To School I'll go, and learn to do
whatever God doth say;

No God but he, that formed me,
I'll worship and obey.

On the Lord's day, I'll read and pray,
and hear God's holy Word;
Whilest I do live, that Day I'll give
up wholly to the Lord.

Adulterie, good men defie;
O 'tis a cursed evil:
And such as to whore-houses go,
must perish with the Devil."

The first two verses provide an interesting anticipation of
the moralistic poetry for children which the two sisters
Ann and Jane Taylor were to make so extraordinarily
popular in the nineteenth century.[9] The last one, with its
reference to "adulterie" and "whore-houses", is a reminder
of a more robust approach to moral education than the
nineteenth century would have thought proper. On this
point also, the Rev. Thomas Smith found it necessary to
remove the "indelicate words" from his 1805 edition of
Dyche's well-known text-book.

Another book from this period which continued in use
for several decades was *Cocker's Accomplished School-
Master; Containing Easy Directions for Spelling, Reading and
Writing English*. There was an illustrated fifth edition in
1703, and an eighteenth edition in 1748. Edward Cocker is
probably better known for his arithmetic book, first
published in 1660, which was popular for many years.

Probably not so long a period of popularity was enjoyed
by some of the other books at this time. In 1701, for
instance, appeared *The Expert English School-Master,* by
Thomas Lydal, "School-master in Canterbury". There is no
copy in the British Museum, but Arber in his *Term Catalogues* (Vol. III) quotes the title-page in full, and the book
is intended "for the ease of the Learner: who, after he is

9.  Their *Original Poems for Infant Minds* was first published in
    1804, and very often reprinted. See G. E. Harris, *Contributions
    Towards a Bibliography of the Taylors of Ongar and Stanford
    Rivers*, London, 1964; D. M. Armitage, *The Taylors of Ongar*,
    Cambridge, 1939.

instructed herein, will be capable of reading the Bible". The same author's *Tables of Words* was also published in 1701. Yet another text-book advertised in 1701, but by an unknown author, was *The School-Master,* which promised "a new method of teaching Children, at three years old, to read and write English".

Occasionally the transcription of a title-page can tell us a good deal about the contents of a book of which no copy appears to have survived. In 1704 an elementary reader for charity schools was published anonymously, and the title-page reproduced by Arber indicates its scope:

"The Charity School, Or Reading and Spelling made easy to the meanest Capacity; chiefly designed for the use of all Charity Schools in England: containing, 1. Tables of Common Words from one Syllable to Eight, divided and not divided. 11. A Catalogue of the proper Names and Places in the Bible, etc. 111. The Church Catechism, etc., for bringing up Children in the Protestant Religion."

Presumably this book, which was reprinted in 1705, was used widely in charity schools. Certainly Thomas Crumpe's spelling book was; it was published in 1712 with a characteristically long title:

"The Anatomy of orthography: or, a Practical Introduction to the Art of Spelling and Reading English, Adapted to mean Capacities. Composed for the Use of English-Schools, and humbly offered to the Masters of the Charity-Schools."

The charity school at Cripplegate, London, made use of Crumpe's book. In the Committee Minutes we find the following entries:

"19 September 1712
Agreed to have fifty of Crumps Spelling Books at 3½ p book . . . ."
"28 May 1714
25 of Crump's Spelling Book ordered @ 3½d. each."

Since this is the first concrete evidence we have of a

particular text-book being used in a specific school, it is worth while to examine this book more closely. The price must have seemed attractive to committee members, and it is possible that this consideration influenced their purchase of it rather than any intrinsic excellence which it might have possessed. In fact, it was an extremely good little manual. Its seventy-two pages led the beginner from the alphabet to words of several syllables, and when the contents had been mastered, the reader was ready, in theory at least, to tackle the catechism and the Bible. The author, a teacher, had clearly given some thought to his compilation:

"... I have experimentally discovered the Necessity of a Book digested in this Method: Because other Spelling-Books beginning with long Monosyllables, which are beyond the Capacity of, and too difficult for young Beginners, render the initiatory part of Learning bitter and unpleasant to them, and consequently the Teacher's Business so troublesome to him, that these Books, seeming very obscure, are generally too much neglected. For my own part, I have been always forced to teach the middle, or latter End of the Common Spelling-Books, before I could bring Children to a Capacity of learning the long Syllables in the former Part; and I commonly teach the long and difficult Monosyllables last of all."

Crumpe's method of teaching reading amounted, then, to a different order for learning the syllables, and he hoped that this rearrangement would be of assistance to other teachers, and would "render the elements of Reading more pleasant and delightful to Children, and speedily encourage them to, and prepare them for further Rules and Instructions set forth in other Books of this Kind". His book was being advertised in the 17th edition of *Methods Used for Erecting Charity-Schools,* published by the Society for Promoting Christian Knowledge in 1718, but no copy of any subsequent edition appears to be traceable.

This apparently limited popularity of Crumpe's book may have been affected by the fact that it appeared three years after a text-book which enjoyed a phenomenal success, and remained in use for upwards of one hundred and twenty years. This was *A Guide to the English Tongue in Two Parts* by Thomas Dyche, published in 1709. A second edition was called for in the following year; there was a 14th edition in 1729, and a 45th in 1764; another edition came out in 1796; it was revised in 1805, and the last edition in the British Museum is the one dated 1830.

Dyche's career as a schoolmaster has already been referred to; and the most noteworthy quality of his book is its thoroughness. The title-page of the second edition indicates its scope and contents:

> "A Guide to the English Tongue. In Two Parts. The First proper for Beginners, shewing a Natural and Easy Method to pronounce and express both Common Words, and Proper Names; in which particular Care is had to shew the Accent for preventing Vicious Pronunciation. The Second, for such as are advanc'd to some Ripeness of Judgement, containing Observations on the Sound of Letters and Diphthongs, Rules for the true Division of Syllables, and the Use of Capitals, Stops and Marks, with large Tables of Abbreviations and Distinctions of Words, and several Alphabets of Instructions for Young Writers."

It is interesting to note that writing is not introduced until well into the second part — very strong presumptive evidence, in view of the book's popularity, that it was normal eighteenth century practice to teach reading before writing was attempted. The dedication "To the Worthy Members of the Society United for the Cloathing and Tuition of an Hundred Poor Boys in the Parish of St. Giles Cripplegate" offers some ground for thinking that Dyche had the problems of charity schools in mind when he wrote his book, though as he says, he hopes it will be of use to other pupils besides poor children.

In a three-page Preface, Dyche discusses his methods, and in this instance the second edition is very much more valuable than the first because he mentions one or two comments which were made by other teachers upon the earlier edition:

> "Many of the Learned have been pleas'd to signifie their Approbation of my main Design, and to confer their

Advice, for which I think both my self and the Publick oblig'd to 'em."

The general opinion was that syllables should be divided by the rules of Latin Grammar, and Dyche followed this rule as far as he was able, though with some reservations: "I must confess that in Teaching Children to read, I think the Ear a better Guide". To support this view Dyche quotes a Mr. Hardistee who wrote to him at length upon this subject, and who mentioned with approval "Comenius's Rule, Two or three Consonants, plac'd between two Vowels must be join'd with that Vowel, which gives the softest sound to the Ear". In order to make this clear, Dyche introduces the symbol ∥ — "which is frequent in almost every Page of the Book" — and uses it in the following way:

"... As for instance, re∥bel, re∥lick, re∥lish, are truly divided by the Rule; but you must sound them reb-el, rel-ick, rel-ish, to comply with the Custom of the Language. And the Learner might be permitted to spell 'em so, if the Teacher please; but with this especial Caution, that in Writing, when a Word is to be parted at the End of a Line, we follow the Rule very strictly and not the Ear."

These comments have been quoted at some length because they reflect the concern of eighteenth century teachers of reading with syllables. The principle of the splitting up of words into syllables was never in doubt; but the methods by which these syllables were split and words were built from them, and the way in which these procedures were to be presented, were regarded as matters for discussion.

Dyche goes on to say that most of the teachers "were of the Opinion, that setting the Words twice over, divided and whole, was unnecessary; and therefore you'll find 'em but once in this Edition". In order to offset what might be a disadvantage in this method, Dyche falls back upon the question and answer method to teach various rules of spelling. He was also aware of the growing number of foreign words coming into the English language, and offered guidance in the pronunciation of both these and various biblical words. His criterion of pronunciation is that of custom rather than correctness — "Custom must be our rule for the Present ...", he says; and he disclaims any errors which are made — "if my Country-men will still fondly pursue their Absurdities, 'tis no Fault of mine".

Altogether, Dyche's Preface shows an. awareness of the problems of teaching reading and of some of the wider issues of language, and his book stood the test of time. In the edition of 1805, which was edited by the Rev. Thomas Smith, comparatively few alterations were made, and these were explained by the Editor:

"... The rapid and extensive circulation of Dyche's Spelling Book, during a long series of years, and the approbation with which it has been received by teachers of the greatest respectability, obviate the necessity of enlarging upon the merits of the original work. Some account, however, may be reasonably expected of the various alterations that have been made in the present edition."

The alterations involved simply the removal of obsolete or indelicate words, the pruning of some of the word lists, and the addition of some new reading passages — for example "The Crow and the Jug" and "The Goose that Laid the Golden Eggs". There was also some poetry by Pope, Cowper, Watts, Shenstone, Gay and Hannah More, intended either for copying or learning by heart; and finally, the reading passages were illustrated by a series of well executed woodcuts. The basic pattern of the book remained unchanged, and Dyche's method was not radically altered — an indication of the lack of development in teaching method during the eighteenth century.

In addition to his *A Guide to the English Tongue*, Dyche was the author of several other books, including *The Spelling Dictionary* and *A New English General Dictionary* (16th edition, 1777).

Thomas Dilworth's *New Guide to the English Tongue* was another popular text-book, and covers very much the same ground as Dyche's work. The earliest edition in the British Museum is the 13th, which was published in 1751, and the book was reprinted in 1836. Despite the evident popularity of this "New Guide", it has proved impossible to discover any details of its author's life, except that he was also the author of *The Schoolmaster's Assistant: being a Compendium of Arithmetic,* which was popular for over fifty years.

One of the cheapest text-books available was Francis Fox's *An Introduction to Spelling and Reading.* At 4d. per copy, or 28s. per hundred, it was likely to appeal to the organisers of charity schools if only because of the price. It was in fact an extremely sound manual which escaped to some extent the dullness of most earlier textbooks, and was not strikingly dissimilar from a chapbook in appearance. The earliest edition in the British Museum is the 7th, which came out in 1754, while in the local history collection at Reading there is a 12th edition, 1785, and a 17th, 1805. Fox, who was born in 1675, was educated at Oxford and died in Reading in 1738, so that his "Introduction" was almost certainly published before this date; and with a 20th edition "corrected and improved" dated 1815, it is clear that this book enjoyed a long period of popularity.

The Preface makes it plain that Fox had written his book with charity schools very much in mind:

> "The method of learning to read here proposed, having been tried with good success in a charity school in the country, it was thought proper to publish it, that each child might have a copy. It was further considered, that what was of use in one school, might be useful in others also."

He continues:

> "As soon as the children know how to distinguish their letters, and have learned the Syllables and Monosyllables, in the beginning of the first part, it is proposed to set them to read the Lessons which follow. And while this is doing; it is proposed that the judicious instructor should, as the children are capable, sometimes teach them the Rules for Spelling and dividing words into Syllables, which are in the second part. These are contained in a

few pages; and therefore may be easily committed to memory."

Fox makes the point that daily practice is important, and stresses the need for close attention to the rules of spelling. Because of his insistence upon this, he explains, the words in the Lessons are not divided into syllables as they usually are "in books of this nature", but the children should be frequently asked by what rule they spell a word, and why they stop at a vowel or consonant when a word is split up. This method, he insists, must be followed until they are thoroughly familiar with the rules.

He goes on to say that when children spell a word, they should not be allowed to guess at part of it: if they are made to spell each syllable in turn, then there will be no difficulty with more difficult words. For further study, Loughton's *A Practical Grammar of the English Tongue* (first published in 1734) is recommended on the grounds of its proved excellence. With regard to the order of the lessons, Fox says that this is arranged "as to convey some necessary knowledge to the minds of children and their parents", and the material has been carefully arranged so that children will find it both "instructive and entertaining".

Two features distinguish Francis Fox's book from the run of eighteenth century readers. First, the alphabet is introduced pictorially with a series of delightful wood-cuts — "Angel; Bull; Cradle; Dog; Eagle, etc.". Secondly, the author shows some concern for the wider issues of reading:

"... Some are of the opinion, that children would sooner come to read English well, if they were not constantly kept to read the Bible, but were sometimes put to read other books."

The books which Fox recommends "to instruct them in particular duties, or to warn them against particular sins" include Ostervald's *Abridgement of the History of the Bible,* 1d.; *Pastoral Advice before Confirmation,* 2d.; *Dr. Woodward against Profane Language.* This is far from suggesting that children should read story books, but it does at least mark the beginning of a move away from the Bible as the sole book to be read; and later in the century Hannah More and Mrs. Trimmer took the task of providing suitable reading matter very seriously indeed.

Before leaving this book, it is worth while looking briefly at the lessons it provides, for they recreate with vividness the atmosphere of a charity school. Part I, consisting of Lessons 1 to 66, is the reading course. In the first six lessons, syllables are dealt with, and in the following lesson words of one syllable are introduced. One of the more advanced reading passages, Lesson 66, is a characteristic blend of difficult words and sound moral instruction:

"Sir Philip Sidney, who was admired and loved for his wisdom and valour all over Europe, his last words were; 'Govern your will and affection by the will and word of your creator: In me behold the end of this world and all its vanities'."

The second part contains the chief rules for spelling and dividing words into syllables. presented as a catechism:

"Lesson IV.
Q. How is ti sounded?
A. When it is neither the first nor the last syllable in the word, and is before a vowel, it is sounded like si or shi, as pa-ti-ent, sounded pashent or pashient."

This is followed by a question on syllables:
"Lesson V.
Q. Is there any general rule for dividing words into syllables?
A. The most general rule for dividing of words into syllables, is to observe carefully the sound or pronunciation of the word."

Towards the end of the book, there is a lesson on words:
"Lesson XV.
Q. How are words divided?
A. Into primitive and derivative; also into simple and compound.
Q. What is a primitive word?

A. A primitive word is a word not derived from another; as man, good, etc.."

The strong influence of the catechitical method upon teaching is apparent in these extracts. Clearly Fox was in deadly earnest when he wrote in the Preface that children should be "frequently ask'd" about the rules of spelling. What could children have made of the distinctions "primitive" and "derivative"? Perhaps in skilled hands the severely formal methods laid down here might have been softened, but it is hard to resist the conclusion that a great deal of elementary instruction in the eighteenth century had as its basis learning by rote, and in many cases the act of learning to read in charity schools seems to have been regarded by pious men as the penance which had to be undergone before the pleasure and profit of reading the Holy Scriptures could be gained.

On the other hand it might be argued that these formal methods simply reflected the serious approach to the problem of teaching poor children to read that is apparent in the text-books of the day. The only touch of lightness, for example, in Francis Fox's book is the charmingly illustrated alphabet already noted.

Another extremely popular text-book made not even this concession to its young readers. This was *A New Grammar* by Anne Slack née Fisher, who was born in 1719 and died in 1778. The second edition of her book – the British Museum has no copy of the first – was published in Newcastle in 1750, and a 22nd edition appeared there in 1801. There were several reprints in London, but most of the surviving copies have a Newcastle imprint. This was the city where Anne Slack lived, and she was married to Thomas Slack, a well-known printer there. Newcastle, after London, was the most important centre of chapbook printing, and it is tempting to speculate upon the connection between this activity and the spread of education amongst the poor on Tyneside. Between 1705 and 1709 four charity schools were established in Newcastle itself, and in 1712 Trinity House School was established by the Master and Brethren for the instruction of children and apprentices. In 1717 the workmen and employers in a local ironworks agreed to set aside a weekly sum of money so that poor children could be taught to read.

It is, then, not surprising that Newcastle should be the place where one of the most successful text-books of the eighteenth century made its appearance.

One of the earliest points made in the introductory lessons is the scope of the term "Grammar". The question and answer method is used:

"Q. What does Grammar treat of?
A. Letters, Syllables, Words, and Sentences."

This answer epitomises eighteenth century practice, and is foreshadowed in "A Letter to the Author on the Method of Teaching" which serves as a preface to the book:

"After the Scholars know their Letters, ground them well in their Monosyllables, with the soft and hard Sounds of C and G, and in what Positions they are so and so ... ; to sound ph as one single character f.. ; to thiz (sic) th thro' the Teeth, like a Greek Theta; this they will soon learn from Word of Mouth, by frequent Repetitions. When they are advanced to Words of more Syllables, let them be us'd to a distinct Pronunciation of each Syllable, with a careful Observation of the Letters that compose it; and as soon as they can spell and divide on Book, they should be put to getting Tables of Words off, and to prove them by Rules ....."

The success of *A New Grammar* prompted its author to write another text-book which went through several editions. This was *The Pleasing Instructor* (Third edition, 1760), and further editions of this were published in Newcastle until at least 1820.

The last of what might be termed the best-selling elementary reading text-books of the eighteenth century was written by John Ash, who was born in about 1724 and died at Pershore in 1779. Ash is perhaps best known as a lexicographer, but the most pleasing of his works was the little school book he wrote entitled *Introduction to*

*Lowth's English Grammar.* Robert Lowth's *A Short Introduction to English Grammar* was first published in 1762 and
was reprinted until at least 1789; John Ash's adaptation of
it for school use first appeared in 1766, and such was its
popularity that seven editions of it were called for in nine
years, and it was reprinted until 1804, when a "Revised,
Corrected and Enlarged" version appeared. It was a straightforward and practical manual, and although the author does
not here provide details of how he considers reading should
be taught, his views upon this important subject are to be
found in his *Sentiments on Education,* 2 Vols., London,
1777 – and in view of the popularity of his text-book, his
ideas are of especial interest.

As is usual in the eighteenth century, the alphabet is the
starting point – "letters are the first elements of all language and learning" – and from here he goes on:

> "When a child has learned the letters, and begins to
> articulate with some degree of ease and propriety, let
> him be taught to distinguish the different sounds of
> vowels, and those of consonants . . . .."

Ash also stresses that children should be taught to read
and spell "by way of diversion". Even more interesting,
however, are his comments upon practices which were
common in the eighteenth century:

> "The old method of dividing syllables begins to be
> deservedly exploded, as contrary, in many instances, to
> the present modes of pronunciation. It seems most
> natural to divide the syllables of a word, however
> compounded, just as we pronounce them. This is an
> obvious rule . . . .."

The text-books of the period, however, show no evidence
that the principle of dividing words into syllables was losing
favour. John Binns, for example, in *The Youth's Guide to the
English Language,* Halifax, 1788, says:

> ". . . When scholars well know the Alphabet, they were
> immediately classed with those who spelled in Mono-
> syllables. They all stood up together every Lesson; the

best Reader began first to spell and the Rest plied the
same words after him . . . ."

The importance of the method of learning to read by
splitting up words into syllables is emphasised by the fact
that the only contemporary criticism of teaching methods
that seems to have survived is for the most part centred
upon this topic. The principle of dividing words into
syllables is not at any time called into question — the
comment deals simply with its application to specific words
and the choice of examples.

The critic was Solomon Lowe, a shadowy figure, of
whom few details have been discovered. He was the author
of several works dealing with theology, education and
language; of these, the study of language appears to have
been his chief interest, and he was the first to propose a
scheme for learning basic French. So "basic" was it that,
according to his *The Whetstone* (London, 1732) "the
grounds of a language may be learn'd in a few hours, so as
to read an author, and write intelligibly". As an example,
he provides a five-page summary of French grammar. The
qualities of directness and even intellectual impatience
which are evident in his proposals for foreign language
learning are emphasised even more strongly in his criticisms
of the authors of various reading text-books, whom he
takes to task in *The Critical Spelling-Book,* published in
London in 1755. In the Preface he justifies this addition to
the many spelling books already available:

"... Teaching to Read is a business of so much importance, and (at the same time) requires so much labour,
skill and attention, even with the best helps; that an
attempt to facilitate the work, it is presum'd, cannot fail
of being acceptable to the public."

It is only the *order* in which syllables are presented to
the pupil which is different in Lowe's book — he attached
great importance to this, and suggested that when words
were divided into syllables, the divisions should be marked
with accents. Unfortunately some of the points he makes
are obscurely expressed and render the theory underlying

his methods very hard to follow. What, for example, is one to make of his comment that the initiation, or early lessons, should "contain only such words as are founded according to the powers of the letters establisht in the alphabet, and syllables pages; which I beg leave to call the primer-powers;"?

After claiming, however, that he has endeavoured to make his own book "incomparably better than any that have yet been offer'd to the nation", he points out that "others have fallen-short of the advantages which would have resulted from a due regard to such sentiments as I have suggested". Who are these other authors, and how does Lowe consider that they have failed to live up to his own standards? As might be expected, there is Thomas Dyche; and his *A Guide to the English Tongue* is criticised as having given -

"... in his first list of dissyllables (p. 17) 140 words; in the first page of which only 17 are to be pronounced according to the rules before laid-down by him for the sound of syllables: and therefore a child (and even a mistress, sometimes) must be at a loss about 123 of them: especially as, for ascertaining the true pronunciation of them, regard must be had to (at least) 12 or 13 exceptions: so that, abating the accent, and the division into syllables, a child might as well begin the art of reading with his bible."

Thomas Dilworth, author of a *New Guide to the English Tongue,* is dismissed as having "little more than copied Mr. Dyche"; moreover, besides reducing the number of monosyllables to be learned, he has disposed them in a curious order, and has confused "Words, whose spelling and pronunciation are different" with those whose "spelling and pronunciation are nearly the same", so that the learner is left with no hints to help him ascertain the sounds of any of them. The instructions given are, claims Lowe, generally confusing and a child will gain little help from them.

*The English Instructor* by Henry Dixon is guilty of all the errors previously mentioned, and in addition his list of syllables and monosyllables amounts to little more than half a page – and even here there are what Lowe calls "diversities of Sound", which he exemplifies by quoting from Dixon's lists:

"all call fall *shall* . . . are care share spare."

The result is "that the confusion, which this mismanagement creates, begins sooner than in the rest of his brethren, and is the more unpardonable, as he has given fewer directions to prevent mistakes".

Also referred to by Solomon Lowe is Mr. Kirkby, author of a *Guide to the English Tongue.* No copy of it is to be found in the British Museum; but a John Kirkby was tutor to Edward Gibbon, and in 1746 he wrote an English and Latin Grammar, so that he may have been the object of Lowe's comment that he is -

". . . so far from having suited his instructions to the capacities of children (for whose use he seems hardly to have designed them) that even scholars will find themselves too much perplext and bewilder'd in a multitude of mazes, to make any great advantage of his guidance."

John Newbery's reading course in *The Circle of the Sciences* is said to give "but an imperfect list of syllables; and even that is of little use to direct in the pronunciation of his tables of words. Thus, in his first list of dissyllables consisting of 40 words, there are but two that can be read on his own principles; and, in that of polysyllables hardly one".

A further target for Lowe's attack is Mr. Pardon, whom he cites as the author of *Spelling New Modeld*[10], and criticises for having given no list of syllables at all; and as if this were not bad enough, Pardon is accused of -

". . . having thrown-together, without any regard but to the number of the syllables, and the order of the alphabet (which last is a matter of little, or no conse-

10. There is no copy in the British Museum. The 3rd edition of Dyche's *A New General English Dictionary,* London, 1740, is described on the title page as "finished by William Pardon".

quence) all sorts of words without any intimation of the difference either of the sound of the syllables, or of the accent of the words."

Lowe's comments upon the work of his contemporaries, stringent as they are, appear to have attracted little attention despite his invitation to readers to communicate their objections to him. His book was reprinted only once; and while to the twentieth century reader many of the points he made appear valid, and his concern to fix "a Standard of the Language" evokes a sympathetic response, the fact remains, if we are to judge from the number of times they were reprinted, that the books he censured such as those by Dyche, Dilworth and Dixon, remained extremely popular. And they were not without competition. Elementary English text-books for use in eighteenth century schools seem to have been offered in profusion; and a study of R. C. Alston's bibliography of spelling books for this period shows strikingly that while a variety of books for elementary instruction in English was available throughout the century, there is an increase in the number of these titles towards its end. It may well be true, moreover, that the size of the editions of well-established books did increase at this time, but we have no means of verifying this supposition. It may also be true that some text-books were printed in very small editions indeed. What is true is that towards the end of the century the text-book trade began to be a separate branch of publishing, as it is today, and the beginning of such specialisation argues for an increased demand for school books. In about 1775, the firm of H. Turpin in London was making a speciality of publishing and supplying text-books to schools and schoolmasters all over England, as an advertisement of the firm at this time makes plain:

"School Books in general are also sold by the said H. Turpin,' and School Masters readily furnished with Allowance, from any parts in Town or Country."[11]

11. See *Publishers' Catalogues,* a unique collection in the St. Bride's Printing Library, London. Item 151 is a catalogue issued by Turpin in about 1775.

Some years later, in 1784, he was advertising children's books and offering "Great allowance to boarding schools in general."

As we shall see in a subsequent chapter, both the Society for Promoting Christian Knowledge and John Wesley realised the need for a system of publishing and distributing books, and they were pioneers in specialised religious-cum-educational publishing. Wesley's *Lessons for Children* was issued in four parts. The first, dated 1746, contains an address "To all Parents and School-Masters", in which Wesley warns against "making children Parrots, instead of Christians" – clearly an echo of Watts' views which had been expressed ten and more years earlier. Another of Wesley's school books was his *Short English Grammar,* which has been most ably and not uncritically analysed by G. H. Vallins in his book *The Wesleys and the English Language,* 1957.

Sarah Trimmer's *The Charity School Spelling Book,* published and distributed by the Society for Promoting Christian Knowledge, is of interest not only for the way the material is presented, but also because it anticipates to a small extent the idea of making school books interesting as well as instructive. It is in two parts; and two versions of Part I exist, one designed for boys, the other for girls, both of which were in a 5th edition in 1799. In its 36 pages this first part gives no explanation of the author's method, presenting simply the alphabet, lists of words, and "Short Stories of Good and Bad Boys in One Syllable only". To these is added advice such as the following:

> "And you should walk back to school in your place, and not run out of your rank, for it has a bad look to see a Boy or Girl run in the street in a rude way."

One of the stories for boys is about Tom Bird, who persisted in throwing stones. After breaking a street lamp he "was put in the cage and beat a great deal"; however, when he blinded Frank Ross in one eye and badly scarred Betsy Sharpe, he merely said he meant no harm, and the author contents herself with a moral!

For girls there is, amongst others, the cautionary tale of

Betty Clarke, who played with fire and was inevitably burned to death.

Part II of *The Charity School Spelling Book* is a much longer volume of 162 pages, and is found in a 4th edition in 1798. This has a short preface which illustrates not only Mrs. Trimmer's practical good sense, but also the way in which teaching methods had remained unchanged throughout the century:

> ". . . To spell is to make use of proper letters to form words; to divide words into syllables; and to give the letters in each syllable their proper sound altogether. A syllable signifies one or more letters expressing a distinct sound. As many different sounds as there are in a word, so many syllables it contains."

Typical of the little stories in the second part is the following:

> "John Gibson is a very honest man, he is by trade a baker of cakes. Children are very fond of cakes; one would not hurt the trade of such a man as John Gibson, but yet it must be owned that money is better laid out in a roll and cheese than on cakes and trash."

Sarah Trimmer was no innovator, and the assumption behind all her tales remains the acceptance of class distinctions; but in one respect she does add interest to her moral stories, in that the characters are charmingly named – and this in itself was quite revolutionary in school books of the period. Giles Gingerbread had for some years been a favourite in children's story books[12]; but the introduction into the classroom of Patty Clive, Charles Frost, Mary Foster, Frank Gilbert, John Knight, Tom Simkins, Becky Bond and others – even in stories of unexceptionable moral worth – must have seemed like a breath of fresh air to children whose early experience of reading at school had been the oppressively long lists of words and syllables that characterised the eighteenth century spelling book.

12. *The (Renowned) History of Giles Gingerbread: a little boy who lived upon learning*. Price 1d. This had been first published by John Newbery in 1765.

What, then, were the general characteristics of eighteenth century text-books? First, the general pattern of teaching children to read – letters, syllables, words, the Bible or similar devotional work – had been set in the earliest school books of the later sixteenth century, and there is no evidence to suggest that this was questioned during the period under discussion. It follows from this that there were no spectacular advances in teaching technique; rather do we see a spread of well-established methods. Neither, with the sole exception of Solomon Lowe, was there any serious attempt made to question the way in which tried techniques were worked out by individual authors and teachers, and Lowe's comments have the appearance of an irritable monologue rather than a serious exchange of views.

Where we do find new developments – developments which were significant for long-term changes in teaching techniques and in school books – they appear to have gone without notice when they were introduced. Three examples can be cited. First, there was the attempt to produce a simple catechism for less able children. The Rev. Simon Ford, as early as 1684, had shown an awareness of this as a need; and reference has been made also to the catechism published by the Diceys mid-way through the century for "such as are of weak capacities". The innovation, however, seems to have been prompted by religious rather than educational needs. Then there was the extremely pleasing appearance of Benjamin Collins' battledores – the first time colour had been used to provide attractive educational material – and also the use of characters with real names in Sarah Trimmer's spelling books. Finally, there was the attempt by John Urmston at the beginning of the century to relate teaching material to the pupil's experiences, an idea which was entirely ignored by his contemporaries and immediate successors.

Generally, eighteenth century text-books were dull in their contents and unattractive in appearance. There were, of course, minor exceptions to this: within the limits of an extremely narrowly based theology, Benjamin Keach attempted to provide varied materials; so too did Francis Fox. The use of illustrations was not widespread – perhaps surprising in view of the fact that woodcut blocks for illustrations could be cut very cheaply, and that most printers in any case would have carried a stock of them; but the inclusion of two illustrations in the Diceys' *ABC with the Shorter Catechism* was most unusual. Furthermore, the edition of Comenius' *Orbis Pictus* which had been re-printed in 1705 demonstrated clearly the educational advantages of a visual approach to learning.

There is, of course, the problem of judging to what extent such text-books were actually used in teaching poor children to read. Before the eighteenth century, text-books would have been used only by the small number of pupils attending Grammar Schools and Free Schools; but in the eighteenth century we find that three of the most frequently reprinted books were written by men closely connected with charity schools. Thomas Dyche and Henry Dixon both taught in them, and Francis Fox in the preface to his book is quite specific about its being intended for use in charity schools. Here, then, is evidence that text-books were widely used in such establishments, and they would probably have been bought from the funds subscribed for the running of these schools, as in the case of the charity school at Cripplegate quoted earlier.

With regard to the provision of books in private venture or dame schools, we enter the realm of conjecture. Where no funds were available, it is unlikely that enough books to equip classes could have been provided. It is possible that a Bible on the teacher's table was the only book used – Hone recalled that the old woman who taught him his letters used the Bible. Another possibility was the horn-book, and after about 1770 the battledore was readily available; but it is not possible to estimate with any certainty the extent of the use of books in private establishments.

There seems little doubt that the charity schools were better off than these other establishments with regard to the supply of books, and while it is by no means certain that every child would have had an elementary reader, there are instances in the records of these schools which indicate that books were taken away when children left. For example, an entry for the 31st October, 1771, in the minutes of the Cripplegate Within Ward Schools Committee states:

> "Agreed that Sarah Reed and Jemima Croydon have leave to quit the School and that they be allowed their Clothes and Books."

Was this a standard practice? There is no means of knowing; but of the availability of a wide range of elementary school books in the eighteenth century there is no doubt at all.

A degree of imprecision attaches to the use throughout this chapter of the word "edition", and something must be said about it. Insufficient evidence exists for an accurate estimate to be made of how many copies comprised one edition of an eighteenth century school book, but there is some indirect evidence to suggest that it was considerable. If we assume an *increasing demand* for reading primers – and in view of the development of charity schools and other agencies of elementary education, this seems reasonable – then printing practice would dictate a high print run for each title. Moreover, at an earlier period, the production of certain text-books was regarded as a lucrative undertaking for which the Crown granted a monopoly. In 1582, John Day complained to the Star Chamber that his patent for printing the *ABC with the Catechism* had been infringed by Roger Ward, who admitted printing ten thousand copies of it. Three years later, in 1585, Day alleged that thirty-five thousand unauthorised copies of the ABC had been issued. These figures are impressive. When we consider that the population of England and Wales rose from 6,000,000 at the beginning of the century to 9,178,980 at the first official census in 1801, and when we bear in mind the expansion in the facilities for basic education that have already been noted, then we have very strong presumptive evidence that the demand for text-books would have been greater than it was at the end of the sixteenth century. We have seen how this demand was met, and can I think assume that successive editions of some books would have been very large indeed.

Despite their shortcomings, and use in hands which were often unskilled, the teaching of reading remained, in an age when the acquisition of this basic skill was subordinated to· the demands of religious education, the most important single subject in the curriculum of elementary schools. The implications of this fact are crucial to an understanding of how literacy spread amongst the poor in the eighteenth century, and they will be examined in detail in the ensuing chapters.

# Chapter 4

## APPROACHES TO LITERACY

Today the term "literacy" implies a degree of proficiency in both reading and writing; but in the past the two arts were sharply divided.[1] It must therefore be emphasised that whilst the ability to write amongst poor people in the eighteenth century and even earlier may be evidence that they had received some kind of elementary instruction, the converse is not necessarily true, and absence of the written word is not decisive proof of an inability to read. In terms of the eighteenth century, therefore, there is justification for defining literacy as the ability to read a book or single sheet printed in English.

Having defined literacy simply as being able to read, we should say something further in general terms about this important skill. In the period we are discussing, it was the crucial element in a pattern of communication which had developed in response to a cluster of needs connected with man's social and economic life. These, as M. M. Lewis has pointed out, originated "partly in the restless inventiveness of man, partly in the basic necessities of his life". The impact made by the written word upon society was twofold: so far as writing made possible the accumulation of knowledge, and tended to fix tradition, belief and patterns of behaviour, it represented a conservative influence. On the other hand, since it promoted a much wider transmission of learning and exchange of ideas, it was a revolutionary force. This aspect of writing was further enhanced by printing – "three thousand years", wrote Lancelot Hogben, "separate the appearance of the first alphabet and the invention of printing with movable type".[2]

1. cf. J. W. Adamson, *The Extent of Literacy in England in the Fifteenth and Sixteenth Centuries: Notes and Conjectures,* (Printed in *The Library,* September, 1929. Reprinted in *The Illiterate Anglo-Saxon,* Cambridge, 1946).
2. *From Cave Painting to Comic Strip,* London, 1949, p. 123.

It is in the light of the development of printing that we seek an answer to the question posed at the beginning of Chapter 1: to what extent was the ability to read widespread amongst ordinary men and women in eighteenth century England?

In order then to do so, it seems most fruitful, after having discussed elementary education in theory and practice, to look at the popular literature of the period which was published specifically for them, and then to examine in detail the section of the book trade, both in London and in the provinces, which provided it. Such an enquiry will not, of course, yield a statistical analysis of readers and non-readers, but it may indicate the existence of a considerable and growing reading public amongst the working class throughout the century.

Thomas Holcroft was born in 1745, and he remembered having seen, as a child, ballad sheets pasted onto cottage and alehouse walls. At the turn of the eighteenth century George Crabbe in his *Poems* offers a glimpse of the books which were to be found in a peasant's cottage. Besides religious works, he writes:

> "Unbound and heap'd those valued tomes beside
> Lay humbler works, the pedlar's pack supplied;
> Yet these, long since, have all acquired a name:
> The Wandering Jew has found his way to fame;
> And Fame, denied to many a labour'd song,
> Crowns Thumb the Great, and Hickathrift the strong.
> There too is he, by wizard-power upheld,
> Jack, by whose arm the giant brood were quelled."

Such books he described as "the Peasant's joy", and these lines may well have been inspired by memories of his childhood, when he visited the cottages of old women in Aldeburgh and rummaged among their shelves for books or ballads.

John Clare describes the books that he saw in a farmer's house at about the same period. There was a Bible, an almanac, *The Whole Duty of Man,* and some chapbooks which he described as "a heap of pamphlets among which was the 'History of Jane Shore', 'The King and the Cobler', 'Johnney Armstrong' and a fragment of an old book on cookery . . . .". He describes, too, the reading of chapbooks by herdboys:

> "Whose ignorance in weary mood
> Pays more regard to robin hood
> And giant blue beard and such tales."

If it can be shown that a reading public amongst the working class did in fact exist, this provides a means of judging with some validity the success of charity schools and private establishments offering elementary instruction. Moreover, the existence of large numbers of readers amongst artizans at the close of the century may well have been of profound significance for the wider issues of working class history at this period.

Any discussion of literacy upon the lines indicated above involves a consideration of two issues. Does the mere existence of books entail a growth in the reading public? And if books were bought, were they necessarily read? To the former question the answer is no — the presence of books does not of itself argue for a growth in readership; but an increase in the book supply suggests strongly the existence of a growing number of readers. If therefore the number of books for the poor, i.e. chapbooks, coming onto the market increased throughout the eighteenth century, then it must be argued that so too did the number of working class readers. There is of course no way of knowing with certainty that the chapbooks bought from pedlars were actually read, but the balance of probability suggests that they were. A penny or halfpenny represented no inconsiderable sum to the poor at this period, and it is unlikely that books which were purchased remained unread. Moreover, there is nothing in the few working class autobiographies of the period to suggest that the possession of chapbooks was in any way unusual or conferred any social standing upon the owner.

The importance of the problem of literacy — in somewhat different terms from those postulated here — has been emphasised by Peter Laslett in *The World we have Lost:*

"... The discovery of how great a proportion of the population could read and write at any point in time is one of the most urgent of the tasks which face the historian of social structure, who is committed to the use of numerical methods. But the challenge is not simply to find the evidence and to devise ways of making it yield reliable answers. It is a challenge to the historical and literary imagination."

While I agree wholeheartedly with the last statement, there are two points here which seem to me to be misleading. The first is the equation of literacy with reading *and* writing, and the second is the insistence upon the use of statistical methods. Initially, as we have seen, literacy involved the ability to read, and failure to distinguish between the two arts of reading and writing leads Mr. Laslett into the error of supposing that literacy in the eighteenth century can be measured in statistical terms by counting the signatures of bridegrooms who, after Hardwick's Marriage Act of 1753, were required to sign the Parish Register, or if they were unable to do so, to make a distinctive mark. Whilst he acknowledges that this is not a very straightforward piece of evidence, he regards signatures in parish registers as likely to be the most important source available.

My objection to this hypothesis is that reading was very much more widely taught than writing, so that there were likely to be numbers of people who could read but who could not write. In all the references to educating the poor, reading is the first subject mentioned: E. P. Thompson in *The Making of the English Working Class* makes the point that there were more readers than writers amongst the working class in the early years of the nineteenth century. The consideration of educational theory and practice in Chapter 2 above suggests that the discrepancy must have been much greater in the eighteenth. Apart from any other consideration, it was very much easier – and cheaper – to teach reading than writing, and once the skill had been acquired it was a much simpler matter to practise it, since there were few if any social compulsions which necessitated the ability to write. Moreover, is it not more than possible that the clergyman, whose responsibility it was to keep parish records, may have guided the bridegroom's faltering hand as he signed his name, or even written the signature for him, so that the letter of the law could be honoured?

In the absence of evidence other than a bridegroom's signature, the problem of ascertaining the extent to which the ability to write was widespread seems intractable, and the statistical approach favoured by Mr. Laslett offers only a partial and unsatisfactory solution. It is also, of course, related to a date as late as 1753, and if evidence regarding literacy earlier in the century is sought, we must look elsewhere.

Even so, what might be termed the demographic method does at least realise the existence of a problem, and attempts to come to terms with it. More usually, the ignorance of the working class in eighteenth century England is assumed without question. In *The Library*, New Series, Vol. I, 1900, for example, A. Clarke wrote of

". . . the gross ignorance of the lower class, among whom reading was a rare accomplishment, and writing almost unknown."

More recently R. D. Altick suggests in *The English Common Reader*, 1957:

". . . it was among the middle class, rather than among the working people, that the taste for reading made headway during the eighteenth century."

Altick speaks of "a low literacy rate among the masses", and although he mentions chapbooks, he appears unaware of the extent to which they circulated; and the bibliography appended to his book ignores some of the more important works in this field.

In *The Rise of the Novel* Ian Watt is equally forthright in asserting that a working class reading public did not exist in the eighteenth century:

" . . . There is much evidence to suggest that in the country many small farmers, their families, and the majority of labourers were quite illiterate, while even in towns certain sections of the poor - especially soldiers, sailors and the rabble of the streets - could not read.

In the towns, however, it is likely that semi-literacy was commoner than total illiteracy."

Such a point of view fails to take account of a great deal of evidence which is presented here. It has been shown that there was some discussion regarding the advisability of teaching the poor to read, and that text-books, catechisms and battledores were readily available for use in charity schools and other humble establishments offering elementary education. Moreover, if it can be shown that chapbooks were printed in increasing numbers and were widely distributed, then it must be assumed that they were purchased and read; and to whom would they appeal except to the urban and rural poor — for middle class readers would have scorned these productions, which belonged to a world far removed from the one where Pope's glittering verse and the urbane prose of *The Spectator* were admired.

What assumptions about the ability of the poor to read were held during the eighteenth century itself? Certainly the pious founders of the Society for Promoting Christian Knowledge had little doubt that amongst the humblest members of society there existed those who were able to read. Proof of this statement is to be found in the programme of tract publication which was initiated soon after the beginning of the Society in 1699. This enterprise has received very much less attention than the charity school movement, but was equally important, and the assumption of literacy underlying the production of tracts addressed to soldiers, sailors, hackney coachmen and others is both novel and significant. The novelty of the endeavour lay in the fact that never before had anyone consciously attempted to reach a wide section of the poorer classes with written pious exhortation; and it was significant because in the prolix and often dull religious pamphlets issued in the early days of the Society we can discern, however dimly, the beginnings of cheap non-fiction publishing — a field of activity which became increasingly important and developed a vigorous secular side throughout the nineteenth and early twentieth centuries.

There is no doubt at all that the question of publishing and distributing tracts was regarded as being second only in importance to the provision of charity schools. At a meeting held on the 22nd of February, 1699-1700, a Mr. Shute, who had been a member of the Society since its inception, suggested that Bibles, prayer books and tracts should be provided for the prisoners in Newgate. Two years later, the possibility of issuing tracts for sailors was discussed:

"... Ordered that S$^r$ John Philips be desired to speak to S$^r$ George Rook about dispersing the Seamen's Monitor, together with the Kind Caution against Swearing, and the Persuasive to the Observation of the Lord's Day amongst the Saylors in his Majesty's Navy."

At the same meeting, eight hundred copies of a tract warning readers against the evils of bad language were supplied to Major Herne for distribution to the hackney coachmen of London. An even more ambitious undertaking was reported by Mr. Serjeant Hook at the meeting of the Society for Promoting Christian Knowledge held on the 16th of June, 1701:

"... the Society for the Reformation of Manners had dispersed above thirty thousand printed Papers throughout all the publick Houses in and about London and Westminster, and that the papers were well received in all these Houses, tho' between six and seaven thousand in number, except in about twenty of them."

The kind of pamphlet which was circulated will be discussed later. What is of interest here is the idea that reformers thought it worth while to circulate such large quantities of their hortatory literature in public houses, and that they assumed that they would be read.

Soldiers as well as sailors were among the recipients of tracts. The Navy appeared to the pious men who met weekly to present an urgent problem, and in the early minutes we find numerous references to dispersing tracts

amongst sailors. A typical reference to this is recorded in
the minutes of the meeting held on the 16th September,
1702:

> ". . . Mr. Barclay moved that a competent number of
> Seaman's Monitors and other of the Society's Papers may
> be Distributed amongst the Seamen on bord the Victory
> in the Harbour at Portsmouth."

No less than six thousand tracts were sent to Holland for
distribution to soldiers there in 1701. The original plan had
been to send five thousand copies of *The Souldier's
Monitor*, but in fact three thousand were sent, together
with three thousand copies of *Pastoral Letters*. Early in
1702 there was a scheme to distribute tracts to all the
soldiers in English garrisons, and later in the same year
three thousand five hundred assorted pamphlets were sent
to the troops in Ireland.

The concern of the Society for Promoting Christian
Knowledge in these matters is beyond doubt. The question
remains: precisely what weight can be attached to evidence
of this kind? Was it simply an indication of the reformers'
lack of realism[3], or were there good grounds for supposing
there to be some degree of literacy amongst the poor? If
we are to judge the members of the Society for Promoting
Christian Knowledge from the point of view of the charity
school movement, the charge of lack of realism can hardly
be sustained. Their early discussions[4] show a lively sense of
reality, and they were hardly likely to waste the money
which they had themselves in large measure contributed, to
finance schemes which were both impractical and chi-
merical.

What is very much more arguable is that an excess of
enthusiasm may possibly have led them to overestimate the

3.  David Owen, in *English Philanthropy 1660-1960* tells us that
    Thomas Firmin, at the end of the seventeenth century, had
    printed ten thousand copies of a scripture catechism for his
    spinners and their children. Firmin's career does not suggest "a
    lack of realism". (See *The Life of Mr. Thomas Firmin* . . . 2nd
    Ed., London, 1791).
4.  See Rev. E. McClure, *A Chapter in English Church History*, 1888.

extent to which their tracts would be read by the public which they most wished to reach. There are, however, one or two pieces of evidence which point to their being perhaps more accurate in their assessment of the reading public than Altick, for example, is prepared to admit.

Firstly, a book which reached a seventh edition in 1703 indicates clearly in its title the public for whom it was intended: *The Compleat Servant-Maid, or the Young Maiden's Tutor. Directing them to qualifie themselves for any of these employments, viz. waiting-women, house-keeper, chamber-maid, cook-maid, under cook-maid, nursery-maid, dairy-maid, laundry-maid, house-maid, scullery-maid.* The title alone provides a splendid example of eighteenth century self-education, and the assumption that maidservants might be able to read such a manual with understanding is an interesting one.

Secondly, there existed at the beginning of the eighteenth century a well established popular literature in the form of printed ballads and chapbooks, for a number of the printers listed in Appendix (ii) were active in this ephemeral publishing at the turn of the seventeenth century. Although I have found no trace in the minutes of the Society for Promoting Christian Knowledge of any discussion of either chapbooks or ballads, it seems unlikely that its members could have been unaware of the extent of this popular literature – many of them were active parish priests.

As early as 1708 popular literature was the subject of sharp criticism: "Throw away all fond and amorous Romances, and fabulous Histories of Giants, the bombast Atchievements of Knight Errantry, and the like ....", wrote the anonymous author of *The History of Genesis,* who deplored such "vain Books, profane Ballads."

The view that the Society for Promoting Christian Knowledge tracts were consciously designed to counteract this kind of literature is found in an anonymous pamphlet, *A Representation of the Present State of Religion,* which was published in 1711, and states that a -

"... great Variety of plain and useful Discourses have been distributed among the meaner Sort for their more easy Improvement."

Elsewhere the freedom of printing since 1693, when restrictions upon the number and locations of printers were done away with, is criticised in outspoken terms:

> ". . . since the Expiration of the Act for restraining the Press; and, thro' the greater Liberty of printing, which thereon ensued, have the Vicious and Profane had more Opportunities to scatter their Papers, for corrupting the Manners of Men."

A foreign visitor to London in 1726 commented upon the reading habits of working men in the capital:

> ". . . All Englishmen are great newsmongers. Workmen habitually begin the day by going to coffee-rooms in order to read the latest news. I have often seen shoe-blacks and persons of that class club together to buy a farthing newspaper."[5]

Such evidence taken in isolation may well be questioned, and the accuracy of the observer impugned, but there are indications that this picture was not altogether misleading. Silas Told, the Methodist, some years later mentioned in his autobiography a working man who could not only read, but carried a prayer-book in his pocket:

> ". . . In July, 1740, Mr. Charles Casper Greaves, the young bricklayer . . . took a Prayer-book out of his pocket, and read a few verses out of the Psalms . . . ."

John Scott, the poet, was helped in his early studies by a master bricklayer who was not only able to read, but had a taste for poetry. This would be in about 1747; and in 1761, John Wesley mentions Patrick Ward, a poacher under sentence of death, who could read. Henry Fielding, in *The Journal of a Voyage to Lisbon,* London, 1755, commented upon the devoutness with which "a common sailor" read

5.  C. de Saussure, *A Foreign View of England in the Reigns of George I and George II.* While this comment is interesting in providing a contemporary picture of literacy, it is somewhat puzzling — what is a "farthing newspaper"? *The True Briton,* for example, published during 1723 and consisting of a single sheet, cost 2d.

prayers to the crew. Samuel Bamford's father was a weaver who was able to read well; and as we have seen, William Lovett was taught to read by his great grandmother who was born within the first quarter of the century.

Further examples of the ability to read amongst working men can be found in the pages of G. L. Craik's *The Pursuit of Knowledge Under Difficulties.* It can of course be argued that such men were exceptional and do not represent the vast mass of working men and women; but the details of readers amongst the poorer members of society add a great deal of plausibility and colour to the comments of a contemporary observer, Thomas Negus, Rector of St. Mary's Church, Rotherhithe. In 1761 he preached a sermon[6] which was afterwards printed, in which he made some interesting points about the extent of literacy amongst the poor. As might be expected, he begins by mentioning books which, he says, are "put into their Hands, which their education enables them to read". From here he goes on to mention the quantity of books distributed each year by the Society for Promoting Christian Knowledge:

" ... They disperse Annually amongst the poorest Sort, some thousands of Bibles and Common Prayer Books, and a Variety of other such religious Books and Tracts, as they have thought most useful for the Improvement of their Understanding and Morals."

Thomas Negus follows this up with an important question, to which he provides an illuminating answer:

"... To what purpose would Books be distributed amongst the Poor, if none could read them? They would be like the sealed Book mentioned by the Prophet ... And how few would be able to read them well, so as to understand them if we had no Charity Schools, I leave you to judge: But by means of these Schools, if well encouraged, and duly increased, it may be hoped there

6. The occasion was the "Yearly Meeting of the children educated in the Charity Schools in and about the Cities of London and Westminster".

will be few poor Families, but what will have in them
good Readers . . . ."

It seems, then, that the efforts of the Society for Promoting Christian Knowledge cannot simply be described as
impractical, and warrant a more careful assessment than has
yet been accorded them.

Another witness to the ability of ordinary men to read
was General James Wolfe, who assumed in his orders that
corporals and serjeants in infantry regiments should not
only be able to read, but to write as well:

> ". . . the orderly corporal of each company is to make a
> report in writing every morning."

Another of Wolfe's orders directed that:

> ". . . the serjeants and corporals are to give in an account
> in writing to the commanding officers of the companies
> of the manner in which the different squads mess."

Although not published in book form until 1768, the
orders quoted refer to the period of Wolfe's command in
Scotland in 1749. By the seventeen sixties, the need to
have non-commissioned officers who had received some
education was becoming increasingly apparent, and Captain
Thomas Simes urged that a serjeant or corporal in each
regiment should be employed to teach private soldiers who
could not do so, and their children, to read and to write.

Simes returned to this theme in *A Military Course for the
Government and Conduct of a Battalion,* 2nd Ed., London,
1777, and recommended that the Serjeant Major should be
"a good scholar"; and of a corporal Simes says:

> ". . . He should have a quickness of comprehension with
> a knowledge of reading, writing and accounts necessary
> to discharge the duty . . . ."

Also interesting is the recommendation that there should
be a regimental school, supervised by the chaplain:

> ". . . It would be highly commendable if he would pay
> some attention to the conduct of a regimental school

and appoint a non-commissioned officer to act as master who is capable of teaching reading, writing, and arithmetic, by whom soldiers and their children should be carefully instructed and a place should be fixed upon for that purpose."

Regimental schools of this kind were not unknown in the eighteenth century; there was one in the Tower of London in 1761, but no details of it have survived. Even more unfortunately, the original documents relating to the Hibernian School, founded in 1789, were lost through enemy action in the Second World War, and these may have thrown some valuable light upon our knowledge of literacy in the Army at this time.

The purpose of this digression concerning education in the Army has been to show that men who were able to read were to be found in the ranks during the eighteenth century[7], and that in order to be promoted, the ability to write was virtually a necessity.

So far we have seen that there existed in certain quarters a positive assumption about the ability of many of the poor to read. The Society for Promoting Christian Knowledge spent a considerable amount of money to provide reading matter for them; and if we are to judge by the efficiency of the Army virtually all over the world in the eighteenth century, it would seem that commanding officers found little difficulty in filling their establishments with corporals and serjeants who could not only read, but write as well[8].

The motives which impelled a soldier to learn to read and to write are clear enough; but what incentive was there

7. Also in the seventeenth, cf. Anthony À Wood's *Life and Times,* Ed. L. Powys, Oxford, 1961, p. 47. Some Parliamentary soldiers are described as having "grammar learning".
8. The amount of reading and writing involved in the day-to-day running of a company or battalion is not always realised by those who are unfamiliar with military procedures. The copying of orders, issue of stores and accounting for them, pay and allowances, must have represented a tremendous problem for military administration in the eighteenth century (no less than in later ones!) which was apparently coped with largely by non-commissioned officers.

in society at large for a person to learn even to read, let alone to write? A very small number of boys would have been affected by the increasing demand for clerks in counting-houses and offices, and in order to answer this question we must look elsewhere than in the direction of economic expansion. The ability to read was not a necessary accomplishment amongst the eighteenth century poor. There was no positive inducement for a man or woman to do so; but since so many boys and girls acquired a rudimentary literacy at school, the ready availability of popular literature may well have made it a simple matter to keep up such skill with a degree of enjoyment.

From the close of the seventeenth century the traditional oral literature of men and women which had persisted largely in the form of ballads and traditional tales since the Middle Ages was becoming to an increasing extent part of a culture which relied upon the printed word for its dissemination[9], and in order to share in it fully, some knowledge of reading was desirable. The complexity of the process by which this occurred is intensified by the fact that much of the oral tradition survived long after printed versions of stories and songs had become established. Despite the difficulties, something must be said about the change from a spoken to a printed popular literature.

Soon after the commencement of printing in England in 1476, we find printers issuing broadsides — single sheets of paper with printing on one side only, which had no pretensions to permanence, and which could be discarded when their contents had been read. Their subject matter was various — proclamations, religion, songs and ballads, even advertisements. Broadsides were the earliest form of printed popular literature. Some of the earliest of them were Indulgences — one is dated 1513 — and the oldest ballad I have traced, "A Balade on Thomas Cromwell", appeared in July, 1540. How widely would such things have been read? There is no way of knowing with certainty, but there appears to have been a considerable public for them, and it

9. Abundant evidence for this is to be found in the Bagford Ballads in the British Museum, and the Douce Additions in the Bodleian Library, Oxford.

is possible to trace the development of broadsides over several centuries. They were the principal means by which popular literature became more and more a concern of printers rather than minstrels and ballad singers; and together with the jest books which delighted Elizabethan readers, they were the forerunners of the eighteenth century chapbook whose wide circulation was indicative of an increasing reliance upon the printed word which characterised the eighteenth century.

Another important line of approach to the problem of reading ability is to consider to what extent ordinary people were exposed to print without their making the conscious effort of purchasing a chapbook or ballad sheet. Or, to put it another way, was there in the eighteenth century any visual background of the printed word that was in any way comparable with the one with which advertising has surrounded modern man in today's industrial society?

In a somewhat different and attenuated form, such a background did exist two centuries ago, and may well have done much to accustom working men and women to a world in which the printed word was playing an increasingly significant part. The elements which comprised it were the fly sheets and tradesmen's announcements which became a feature of the larger towns; the fashion for epitaphs in verse upon tombstones; posy-rings and sundial mottoes; and an increasing use of wrapping papers which incorporated the name and address, and often the trade mark, of the merchant from whom the goods had been acquired. Each in its different way brought the ordinary man and woman into contact with print.

In 1762 when the tradesmen's signs which had for so long been a feature of London streets were abolished, shopkeepers who for generations had relied upon a sign to advertise their premises and wares were forced to use printed notices and announcements above the door or window of a shop. An engraving in *Wit's Magazine,* 1784, provides an illustration of a London street in this year. Not only is the street clearly marked as "Milk Street", but there are sheets pasted on the wall advertising May-day celebrations and a "Pantheon Concert". A pewterer's shop is defined by the owner's name and craft across the top of the window, and next door there is a barber, offering a shave for a penny and "A Room for Ladies". Contemporary prints such as those in the Collection at the Guildhall, London, provide further examples of the increasing public use of the printed word after 1762.

Dwellers in the country were not so cut off from print as might be suspected. The parish church, centre of so much communal life in a pre-industrial society, would be surrounded by the churchyard in which local inhabitants were buried, and the taste for finely engraved tombstones ensured that church-goers on their way to or from church would come into contact with the printed word. The length of some epitaphs[10] — written occasionally in verse — would provide reading matter of a kind.

Not all such memorial stones were erected in memory of the wealthy or the famous. Outside Winchester Cathedral stands a memorial to Thomas Thetcher, a grenadier in the North Hampshire Militia "who died of a violent Fever contracted by Drinking Small Beer when hot the 12th of May, 1764. Aged 26 Years." His comrades in arms subscribed to pay for the memorial stone, which includes the following verse:

> "Here sleeps in peace a Hampshire Grenadier,
> Who caught his death by drinking cold small Beer.
> Soldiers be wise from his untimely fall
> And when ye're hot drink Strong or none at all."

This was not an isolated example. Francis Grose, the antiquary, collected a number of epitaphs, some of which he published in *The Olio*, 1792. One is clearly addressed to the passer-by:

> "Halt, soldier, pass not by in such a hurry!
> Here lies a serjeant of the royal Surry;
> John Dennis nam'd, a portly grenadier,
> Whom all the privates did both love and fear."

10. See T. J. Pettigrew, *Chronicles of the Tombs*, London, 1857, and H. E. Norfolk, *Gleanings in Graveyards*, London, 1861. Both books — despite depressing titles — provide many examples of this kind of "churchyard literature".

Grose provides other examples, one couplet commemorating a sailor, one on a dyer and one on a taylor. A rough humour is to be found in the epitaph "On a disorderly fellow named Chest":

> "Here lies one Chest within another;
> That chest was good that's made of wood;
> But who'll say so of t'other?"

Unfortunately the source of the epitaphs is not always given, but the scope of Grose's collection is wide, and there is no reason for supposing that a number of epitaphs did not constitute a kind of popular poetry that existed in a more substantial form than that of the broadside ballad.

Sundial Mottoes, though sometimes engraved in Latin, provided another way of experiencing the printed word; and a book published in 1737 gives examples of sixty mottoes that were in use during the eighteenth century[11]. It is not too fanciful to suppose that they may have been spelled out by gardeners and maids who worked for the families in whose gardens the sundials were set. A motto like the following would hardly be said to tax the skill of one who had learned his letters at school:

> "Amende today and slack not
> Dethe cometh and warneth not,
> Tyme passeth and speketh not."

A more personal awareness of the printed word is to be found in the custom of exchanging rings with rhymes engraved upon them. Such rings are found as early as classical times, and by the sixteenth century it had become a commonplace that rings with a tiny verse inscribed upon them should be exchanged between lovers, and the "posy rhyme" had become an established part of literature. In the early years of the seventeenth century, as John Evans has described in *English Posies and Posy Rings* (Oxford, 1931), "posies were everywhere: on fruit trenchers, on knives, on

11. C. Leadbetter, *Mechanick Dialling: or, The New Art of Shadows,* London, 1737. The mottoes are reprinted in A. H. Hyatt, *A Book of Sundial Mottoes,* London, 1907.

girdles and garters, on poke-dials, on brooches, and on
memorial rings as well as love and marriage rings. No gift
between lovers was complete without a motto to accompany it", and it was not until the close of the eighteenth
century that posy rings began to go out of fashion.
Shakespeare refers to the custom in the *Merchant of
Venice*:

> "About a hoop of gold, a paltry ring
> That she did give me, whose poesy was
> For all the world like cutlers' poetry
> Upon a knife, Love me and leave me not."

To establish the popularity of such verses is one thing; to
relate it to the social life of the eighteenth century poor is
another. There is some reason to suppose that the exchange
of rings between lovers was a commonplace even amongst
the more humble members of Augustan society, for selections of "posy rhymes" formed the subject matter of
several chapbooks. One of these, *Cupid's Poesies,* was
printed in London in 1674, and *The Academy of Compliments* appeared in 1685. This title was later reprinted by
the Diceys, who subsequently issued yet another collection,
*The Best and Compleatest Academy of Compliments.* A
fourth edition of *A New Academy of Compliments* appeared
in 1715 under the imprint of C. Bates and A. Bettesworth,
both of whom were chapbook printers.

The publication of collections of "posy rhymes" in
chapbook form points to their popularity, and to the fact
that they were an established part of eighteenth century
popular culture. It is perhaps not too fanciful to suppose
that the choice of such a motto or rhyme might involve
recourse to a printed source rather than to an oral tradition. Moreover, the quality of these little verses strongly
suggests, with their simple direct statement, that they are
of the same provenance as the ballads which continued to
delight generations of unsophisticated listeners and readers,
and represented a world of feeling which was far removed
from the conscious artistry and elaborate technique of
Pope.

"In constancy, I'll live and die"
"Love is here, Both plain and clear"
"My eyes did find, my heart made choice.
Of her who makes me now rejoice"

[The ring with this last verse was apparently worn by a fishwife in Bath.]

From such trifles as these one cannot argue for an ability to read; but it can I think be claimed that the widespread popularity of posy rings and the quality of their engraved verses indicates that here was one further way in which unlettered men and women might be exposed to the printed word in an idiom that was part of their day-to-day experience.

Printed wrapping papers present a very much more difficult problem. The supremely ephemeral nature of such material makes it difficult to say with accuracy when it was first used. The earliest surviving examples of printed wrapping paper are to be found in John Johnson's Collection of Printed Ephemera at the Bodleian Library, Oxford, and in the John Bagford Collection in the British Musueum. There is also, in the possession of The Imperial Tobacco Company (of Great Britain and Ireland) Ltd., a collection of eighteenth century tobacco labels and wrappers. It was formed by Ingham Foster, who died in 1786, and is probably the most comprehensive assemblage of trade labels and wrappers from this period to have been made. It illustrates the way in which early tobacco merchants relied upon illustrations as well as words, very much in the way of their modern successors.

One final aspect of the background of the printed word remains to be considered. This is the use of tradesmen's tokens as a medium for political propaganda during the last decade of the eighteenth century. Token money has a long history stretching back at least to the reign of Edward I, and tokens were issued by firms and individual tradesmen to fulfil a need for small change which the Royal Mint failed to meet. Amongst the numerous producers of tokens during the eighteenth century was Thomas Spence, a Newcastle man who settled in London. His tokens, which were issued from about 1790 onwards, were designed to be used not only as currency, but also as a means of publicising his highly individualistic radicalism.[12] His propaganda on tokens consisted of illustrations with suitable captions. One of them, issued in 1795 to celebrate the acquittal of Daniel Eaton from a charge of sedition, shows a cock crowing over pigs in a sty with the legend "*Printer to the majesty of the people*", and on the other side a bust of Eaton, and the words "*D. I. Eaton three times acquitted of sedition*". Another shows a North American Indian standing with an axe and a bow. The legend reads "*If rents I once consent to pay/my liberty is past away*". Whatever may be thought of its quality, this material was relevant to the concerns of radicals, and it does indicate one more way in which men were made aware of the printed word.

Yet when such evidence as exists has been examined, we are still faced with a lack of precise information. The extent of literacy amongst the poor can be judged only by inference. It has, for example, been established that the circulation of provincial newspapers went up in the late seventeen thirties and this clearly implied an increased number of readers; but there is no way of telling from which class in society they came. If, then, we are to make valid inferences about the reading public which existed amongst the poor, they must be based upon more solid evidence than that provided by newspapers. Such evidence can be found in the only kind of literature designed for the poorer classes, namely chapbooks. The mass of material regarding their origins and production has been scarcely documented, let alone used within an educational context in an endeavour to answer the important question as to how far the under-privileged members of society two hundred years ago were able to read. This chapter has shown that some of the views quite widely held on this

12. See P. Mathias, *English Trade Tokens,* London, 1962: J. Atkins, *The Tradesmen's Tokens of the Eighteenth Century,* London, 1892; O. D. Rudkin, *Thomas Spence and his Connections,* London, 1927; C. Brunel and P. M. Jackson, *Notes on Tokens as a Source of Information on the History of the Labour and Radical Movement, Part 1,* Society for the Study of Labour History Bulletin No. 13, Autumn, 1966, pp. 26-36.

question may well have been misconceptions, and suggested the most fruitful sources of evidence now available to answer the question. In the chapters which follow an attempt will be made to find the answer.

# Chapter 5

## CHAPBOOKS: ORIGINS AND DISTRIBUTION

### 1

Chapbooks were the small paper-covered books which were offered for sale by itinerant merchants, pedlars and hawkers, often referred to as 'chapmen'[1], throughout the eighteenth century. The wandering merchant, however, had been a familiar figure on English roads long before this period, and from early times he had been the object of more or less repressive legislation which was designed to control vagabonds. A statute of Queen Elizabeth, for instance, refers to "juglers, pedlars, tynkers and petye chapmen" in far from complimentary terms. Nevertheless, at a time when there were few shops outside the towns, the chapman fulfilled a useful social function as a kind of travelling shopkeeper, selling those wares like needles, pins, thread and ribbon which would be required from time to time in every household. In addition to these domestic goods, an important part of his stock in trade by about seventeen hundred had become a budget of small books, priced usually at one penny each.

These little books – chapbooks or 'penny histories' as they were called – circulated in their thousands throughout the Kingdom during the eighteenth century. No satisfactory history of them has yet been written, and the following account of chapbook origins is in no way designed to fulfil this need; its aim is to show briefly how chapbooks developed. From the point of view of the historian of education, the most crucial aspect of chapbook literature is that of the trade; and a detailed study of this may help to answer the central question as to whether the teaching of reading to poor children achieved such success that it created an embryonic reading public of considerably greater extent than has previously been supposed, whose appetite for cheap literature was initially satisfied by chapbooks. For

1. The origin of the prefix 'chap' is uncertain. It may have been derived from the Anglo-Saxon 'ceap', or possibly it was simply a corruption of the word 'cheap'.

this reason the trade is scrutinised in considerable detail in Appendix (ii).

It is difficult to write with complete accuracy of chapbook sources. To trace them in detail would require a meticulous study not only of the origins of fiction, but also of the survival of Medieval romance and the continuing popularity of Tudor jest books — neither of which in their original form had been intended to reach other than a middle class audience — together with ballads and other elements in the traditional oral lore of England's peasantry, for chapbooks preserved in print the remains of a folk tradition whose origins are lost in pre-Christian antiquity.

A consideration of the most popular chapbook titles will illustrate clearly the diverse origins of this ephemeral but important and widely circulated literature. Amongst the favourite titles which are descended from Medieval romance are "Guy of Warwick", "Valentine and Orson", "Bevis of Southampton", "Don Belliaris", "Seven Champions" and "Seven Wise Masters". These were the romances which, as Sir Walter Scott said, "fell into disrepute, though some of the more popular, sadly abridged and adulterated, continued to be published in chap books as they are called."[2]

The process by which a romance of the Middle Ages became a chapbook can be illustrated by reference to one of them, "Guy of Warwick", whose popularity in one form or another lasted into the nineteenth century. Several manuscript versions exist, and printed editions appeared shortly before 1500.[3] One of these, probably issued by Richard Pynson, contained an account of Guy's adventures which, although abridged, was almost identical with a fourteenth century manuscript version in short couplets. The romance was several times reprinted — by Wynkyn de

2. *Essays on Chivalry, Romance, and the Drama,* London, 1887, p. 106. There is a considerable literature on the subject of Medieval romance, but no single work which covers the field adequately. L. A. Hibbard (Loomis), *Medieval Romance in England,* New York, 1924 (New Edition, New York, 1963), is useful. See also G. Ellis, *Specimens of Early English Metrical Romances* (Revised by J. O. Halliwell), London, 1848; A. Johnston, *Enchanted Ground,* London, 1964, which contains a valuable introductory chapter and bibliography.

3. I am indebted to R. S. Crane's study, *The Vogue of Guy of Warwick,* for many of the references which follow.

Worde, by John Cawood, and by William Copland whose edition was illustrated. These versions, rudely printed in black letter, appear to have been designed to reach as wide a public as possible amongst those who at that time were able to read.

Despite some criticism, the fiction of the Middle Ages continued to find favour with readers, and in 1592 the tale of "Guy of Warwick" was published as a broadside ballad by Richard Jones, who specialised in this kind of production. The ballad "A plesante songe of the valiant acts of Guy of Warwick, to the tune of 'Was ever man soe tost in love' ", achieved instant popularity and was constantly reprinted, reaching the kind of public for whom Shakespeare's Autolycus catered. "I love a ballad in print . . . .", said Mopsa in *The Winter's Tale* (Act IV, Sc. III) and although the pedlar does not mention this particular title, the story of the Knight of Warwick would probably have been amongst his "many parcels of charge".

The first verse is typical of the whole production:
  "Was ever Knight for Lady's sake,
  So tost in love, as I, Sir Guy;
  For Phillis fair, that Lady bright,
  As ever Man beheld with eye;
  She gave me leave my self to try,
  The valiant Knight with shield and spear,
  E're that her love she would grant me,
  Which made me venture far and near."

The remainder of the ballad told of Guy's adventures in Normandy and Germany, his victory at Constantinople, his rescue of a lion from a dragon's jaws, his marriage to Phillis and his subsequent desertion of her forty days later, his exploits as a pilgrim in the Holy Land, the return to England, the battle with Colbrond, and then retirement to a cave near Warwick and eventually his death. The anonymous writer of the ballad would have found all this material in printed editions of the old metrical romance, and he added to it the story of the Dun Cow, a fierce animal who according to popular tradition ravaged the Warwickshire countryside.

Other versions of this tale appeared throughout the seventeenth century, all by authors whose names are now forgotten, notably Samuel Rowlands, Martin Parker, John Shurley and Samuel Smithson. By about 1681 "The Famous History of Guy Earl of Warwick" appeared as a small book of twenty-four pages, printed in black letter — clearly a forerunner of the many chapbook versions which were to be printed and reprinted throughout the eighteenth century. At least one version was published in the nineteenth century — the present writer has one dated 1841.

Judging from the frequency with which this title appears in publishers' lists, it must have been one of the most popular chapbooks. It has been discussed here because it demonstrates how Medieval romance designed for a courtly audience had become by the eighteenth century the material of popular literature designed for the lowest class of adult readers, and for children. The processes by which this transformation took place lie outside the scope of the present enquiry; so too does the more general question of the extent to which the Romances of the Middle Ages survived in one form or another up to the Romantic Revival.[4] Their survival in chapbook form was summed up by Lord Ernle in *The Light Reading of our Ancestors,* 1927:

"... Two centuries later (i.e. from 1597) in the debased form of chap-books, knights-errant still roamed the country among the laces and ribbons of the pedlar's pack ...."

Charles Knight commented, too, upon the "Seven Champions of Christendom" and "The Wise Masters of Greece" becoming "vulgar", and in *The Old Printer and the Modern Press,* 1834, he mentioned chapbooks in villages.

Various Tudor jest books continued to be reprinted as chapbooks, and provided the material for such titles as "Joaks upon Joaks", "Groats-Worth of Wit", "Whetstone for Dull Wits" and similar collections. One of the most

4. The literature on the subject is sparse. See E. R. Wasserman, *The Popularity of Elizabethan Prose Fiction in the Eighteenth Century.* printed as an Appendix to his *Elizabethan Poetry in the Eighteenth Century,* University of Illinois Press, 1947, pp. 253-259; and A. Dickson, *Valentine and Orson,* New York, 1929, which traces in detail the fortunes of this romance which became a popular chapbook.

popular Elizabethan light novels dealt with the exploits of Long Meg of Westminster. The earliest (? the first) edition of her adventures was published in 1582 under the title "The Life and Pranks of Long Meg of Westminster", and the immediate popularity of this book is made clear by the numerous references to Long Meg by writers of the period, Thomas Nash, Gabriel Harvey and Ben Jonson to name only three. In Holland's *Leaguer,* 1632, there is a reference to a house kept by her at Southwark, and Henslowe's *Diary* mentions a play called "Longe Mege of Westmester" as having been acted in 1595. During the eighteenth century chapbook versions were printed, and her popularity as a character is finally attested by a reference in Francis Grose, *A Provincial Glossary* (1787), to a proverb: "As long as Megg of Westminster", whose origin Grose traces to "an old fictitious story of a monstrous tall virago ... of whom there is a small penny history, well-known to school-boys of the lesser sort."

The chapbook is an abridgement of the Elizabethan version, and the following brief extracts illustrate its quality. Chapter XVI of an edition published in 1635 includes the following:

". . . After her marriage she kept a house of her own, and lodging and victuals for gentlemen and yeomen, such and so good, as there was no better in all Islington, for there then she dwelt. Now for that often times there resorted gentlewomen thither, and divers brave courtiers, and other men of meaner degree, her house was spoken of: and on one time the constable came to search, and would not be answered what guests she had, but needs would be an eye-witness. Whereupon Meg in a great choler started up in her smock, and taking a strong cudgel in her hand, opened the door for the constable."

In the chapbook published by Dicey, this becomes the final chapter, No. 13:

". . . After marriage she kept a house at Islington. The Constable coming one night, he needs would search Meg's house, whereupon, she came down in her shift with a cudgel . . . ."

Not only was abridgement necessary in order to fit the tale into twenty-four small pages of a chapbook – and if this proved impossible then episodes in the original were simply omitted, as in the case of Long Meg – but the chapbook was also presented in simpler words. The quality of the prose and the vocabulary were such that anyone who had attended on elementary school and shown some aptitude for the basic instruction offered could without too much difficulty have followed the general sense of the tale. If – as so often happened – it was a traditional one, known to the reader in the first place from an oral source, then the task was perhaps easier, since familiarity with the spoken version of a story may have made its appearance in print seem part of a natural process. Further weight is attached to this argument when we recall that collections of popular ballads and songs were often printed in chapbooks called "Garlands". Moreover, some of the most frequently reprinted prose narratives like "Chevy Chase" and "The Blind Beggar of Bethnal Green" were themselves founded upon the known ballads of an earlier period. Tales of Robin Hood, a notable chapbook character, were almost invariably adapted from the ballad versions of his adventures which had enjoyed a popularity lasting over several centuries.

From Robin Hood it is a short step to other chapbook heroes, Tom Thumb, Simple Simon, Jack Horner, Tom Hickathrift, some of whom are still part of a living tradition amongst younger children. The origins of such heroes are unknown, and they belong to the vast mass of English folk-lore which provided the material for so many chapbooks. A very large number of books printed by Dicey and other publishers drew upon the traditional oral lore which had been a part of the life and background of the English peasantry for as long as men could remember. Besides the traditional heroes, there were books which despite titles like the "High German Fortune Book", and the "Egyptian Fortune Teller", were essentially English in their contents. "Nixon's Cheshire Prophecy", "Moles and Dreams", "Mother Bunch" and "Mother Shipton" all catered for a wish to explain dreams and omens besides telling fortunes. Fairies, too, were a part of chapbook literature, and Dicey's edition of "Fairy Stories" was one of the earliest of such collections, the popularity of which has survived into the twentieth century, and shows no sign of diminishing. This element in chapbook literature of superstition and the imagination is one that merits detailed investigation, for in any reconstruction of the world of the eighteenth century the values, assumptions and attitudes of the poor are important, and the only clue to them exists in the books which they read, and which often enshrined their own oral lore.

There were also a few chapbook titles which were unauthorised abridgements and adaptations of works by authors whose names were often not acknowledged by the printers or the unknown hack writers who reduced Defoe's "Robinson Crusoe", "Moll Flanders", or Deloney's "Jack of Newbury" and "Thomas of Reading" to twenty-four page editions. Even Chaucer's "Canterbury Tales" was offered for sale by Dicey, and "Aesop's Fables" was advertised by the same publisher in a catalogue which was printed in 1764.

Amongst the miscellaneous chapbooks were several popular ones — "Dr. Faustus", "Fortunatus" and "Friar Bacon" — which had German origins. There were several unsectarian religious titles; there were those which dealt with crimes or strange happenings ("World Turned Upside Down"); and at least one title presented "Songs in the Beggar's Opera".

The foregoing account — albeit a brief one — of chapbook origins has merely touched upon the immense variety of titles which were available, and has attempted to outline some of the major sources from which this considerable literature sprang. The main element was that of folk lore, and this fact provides a clue to the principal characteristics of these little books. They were unsophisticated, and this lack of sophistication ensured that they would be received with sympathy and pleasure by readers who, as we have seen, were often already half familiar with some of the subject matter before it had appeared in print.[5] The bare ability to read created a growing demand which publishers and printers were able to satisfy with chapbooks which drew upon much that was both oral and traditional; and where novelty was attempted, this was rarely developed very far.

Chapbooks, then, represented an ancient tradition which had become petrified in print: they constituted a vital link in a genuine popular culture. By the end of the eighteenth century they had served their purpose, and adult readers had outgrown them. For the historian they remain a window into the world of common people two centuries ago, through which we may discern not only the extent to which ordinary men and women could read, but also something of their culture.

## II

> "We have choice of songs, and merry books too,
> All pleasant and witty, delightful and new,
> Which every young swain may whistle at plough,
> And every fair milk-maid may sing at her cow.
> > Then, maidens, etc."
> > "The Pedlar's Lamentation", circa 1700.
> (Roxburghe ballads, Ed. J. P. Collier, London, 1847,
> p. 306).

The pedlar or chapman mentioned at the beginning of this chapter had been a familiar figure in the Middle Ages, and a sixteenth century writer mentioned "the Countenance and Tongue, through which they look so saddely and speak so eloquently". Paul Mantoux, in *The Industrial Revolution in the Eighteenth Century,* describes him:

> ". . . The pedlar, his pack on his back or leading a pack-horse, visited all the villages and farms. Not only did he

5. I refer here to the oral tradition, and especially to the fact that ballads were sung and listened to throughout the eighteenth century. John Clare's father, for example, boasted that he could sing over a hundred of them *(Sketches in the Life of John Clare Written by Himself,* London, 1931, p. 46). See also R. Bell, *Ancient Poems Ballads and Songs of the Peasantry of England,* London, 1857; and Willa Muir, *Living with ballads,* London, 1965.

sell scissors and spectacles, coloured handkerchiefs and calendars, but stuffs, fancy leather goods and watches and blocks, in fact everything which the village wheel-wright and blacksmith could not make. He went every-where."

Of his importance during the eighteenth century in bringing chapbooks to towns and villages where there were no book-shops, and to isolated farms, there can be no doubt.

Evidence of the activities and the extent of this wan-dering fraternity of merchants is to be found, not in the meagre records left by chapmen themselves, but rather in the books which were published for their guidance. For his journeys all over the country the pedlar would clearly find essential some kind of road-book, indicating routes and the dates of fairs; and many of these were published. In *The Road Books and Itineraries of Great Britain*, Cambridge, 1924, Sir G. H. Fordham lists the earliest as appearing in 1570, but towards the end of the seventeenth century and throughout the eighteenth they were issued in increasing numbers.

The work of John Ogilby, the seventeenth century topographer, formed the basis of two popular guides, one of which had reached an 11th edition by 1752, and another a 24th in 1794. There were various guides which mentioned chapmen in the title. *The English Chapman's and Traveller's Almanack* was published yearly from 1696 to 1712; and the kind of information contained in such books is set out on the title page of *The Traveller's and Chapman's Daily Instructor*, London, 1705:

"... The High-Ways and Roads and how to Travel from one Place to another. The Market-Towns and the Days of the Week whereon they are kept. All the Fairs in England, Scotland and Ireland; the Time and Places when and where held . . . .
An exact account of all the Stage-Coaches, Waggoners and Carriers . . . ."

Fordham's book lists eighteen titles, excluding reprints, which would have been of use to chapmen as well as to other travellers; and many of them were reprinted several times. Daniel Paterson's *A Travelling Dictionary* came out in 1772, and on 8th edition appeared in 1779. John Cary's two books, *Cary's Traveller's Companion* 1790, and *Cary's New Itinerary,* 1798, were both reprinted soon after publication.

We know sadly little of the chapmen themselves – those who used these books, and whose livelihoods depended upon their ability to travel the country by the most expeditious route. Samuel Bamford in *Early Days,* 1840, wrote a description of the hawkers recalled by his grandfather in 1745:

> ". . . It was customary in those days for Scotch hawkers to travel slowly and laboriously from town to town – not affecting the gentleman as they do at present – but carrying huge and weighty packs on their backs, some four feet in length and two or more in depth – as large in fact as a family meal ark – and stowed with hosiery, drapery, and other necessary articles."

Two brief references to chapmen illustrate the elusive quality of evidence relating to them. According to C. A. Federer in *Yorkshire Chap-books*, 1889, it was a chapman called Isaac who was instrumental in obtaining a well paid post in York for Thomas Gent, who became a celebrated printer in that city; and T. Simpson, the celebrated eighteenth century mathematician, was given his first elementary textbooks by a pedlar.

A more authentic view of chapmen is presented in an obituary notice from an unknown source, dated 1751:

> "Last week died, of a short illness, William Urquhart, a well-known travelling chapman, who, without noise or hurry, without horse or packs, without fraud or dishonesty, acquired about £500 sterling, most of which was found in bank notes and good bills at his death . . . ."

The author then goes on to discuss the role of a chapman in more general terms, "tramping away on his rounds day by day; and attending the yearly fairs in his district", and mentions the fact that chapbooks were a part of his stock in trade.

The parents of Thomas Holcroft were pedlars for an unspecified period during the seventeen fifties, and he refers to this episode in his life in the autobiography he wrote:

"... From the vicinity of Cambridge, we passed on to the Isle of Ely, hawking our different wares, pins, laces, tempting ribbons, and garters in every village we came to; arriving first at Peterborough, and afterwards taking care to be present at Wisbech Fair. Markets, fairs, and wakes, were indeed the great objects which regulated all our motions."

Little, it seems, can be said with certainty of eighteenth century chapmen, and the importance of their achievement in distributing chapbooks is out of all proportion to the obscurity which now surrounds them. They were an essential link between printer and public in days when bookshops were few.

# Chapter 6

## OTHER CHEAP LITERATURE

Apart from chapbooks, the only cheap literature widely disseminated amongst the poor at this time was of a religious nature, and consisted of tracts. Of these, many were in fact distributed without charge by philanthropic people of all kinds to the poor who were deemed to need the comfort and spiritual guidance which these publications were thought to offer.

At the outset of any discussion of eighteenth century popular literature it must be emphasised that chapbooks – being a commercial proposition for printer, publisher and seller – had to be purchased, while religious tracts in most cases were given away. The assumptions made by the pious founders of the Society for Promoting Christian Knowledge and their successors about the ability of many poor people to read are, therefore, of interest and relevance to our study, but it would seem that the evidence of the production and distribution of chapbooks, in response to what proved to be a growing public demand, is a more reliable guide to the extent and increase of literacy amongst the poor than the handing out of tracts – for the latter, if we are to judge by the contents which were often unspeakably dreary, may well have been not only unasked but also unread.

It is generally true that in books designed for mass circulation fiction is a more significant element than theology, however well intentioned; moreover, in a comparison between the secular and religious popular literature of the eighteenth century, differences in visual appeal are immediately apparent. Chapbooks were presented simply and directly, and their illustrations made them attractive to the eye: the unillustrated tracts were often closely printed, their contents prolix, and they appear now to have had little to offer except the undoubted moral fervour of their authors. Towards the end of the century the philanthropist, Hannah More, saw clearly that if theology and morality were to be made palatable for the most unsophisticated readers, they must be suitably disguised; and this led to the production of her "Cheap Repository Tracts", which were illustrated and which offered spiritual and moral guidance in a fictional framework — but her approach was exceptional.

Only a few tracts were issued by private individuals, and with the exception of Hannah More's "Cheap Repository Tracts", none that I have seen differed in any respect from the general run of this kind of publication. T. Green, a Leicestershire Vicar, wrote *Instructions for the Poor;* there was a 5th edition in 1759, and it sold at 3d. per copy or 20s. per 100. An anonymous author purporting to be "a Day Labourer in Lincolnshire" wrote *The Farmer's Advice to his Children,* which was published in Hull, without a date. Also anonymous was *A Treatise on Happiness,* London, 1759 — "4d. or 3s. per dozen to those who give them away", says the title-page. The burden of these tracts is that the poor ought to be content with their humble lot, and they are unattractive in both content and appearance.

Tracts were also issued by the Methodists — who were, however, somewhat tardy in undertaking this kind of evangelical activity; but it was the Society for Promoting Christian Knowledge which dominated the field of tract publishing during the eighteenth century. The sources for a study of their titles are abundant. In the first place, some are catalogued in the British Museum under their authors' names; even more valuable, there is a twelve-volume collection of these publications, issued by the S.P.C.K. in 1800, also to be found in the British Museum; and finally, a surprisingly large number of the Society's catalogues are extant, providing a unique view of its publishing activities.

An early author of S.P.C.K. tracts was Josiah Woodward, who was educated at Oxford, and became a D.D. in 1700. Subsequently he became Minister of Poplar in London, and later of Maidstone in Kent. He was an early member of the Society, his application to join having been approved on the 18th May, 1699, and he was soon concerned in the foundation of a charity school in Poplar. At a meeting held on the 21st July, 1701, it was "Ordered that Mr. Hodges be desired to speak to Dr. Woodward to compose a small Tract for the use of the Souldiers". Woodward would already have been known to churchmen as an author, his *An Account of the Rise and Progress of the Religious Societies in the City of London* having reached a second edition in 1698. A short passage from this will indicate the zeal which inspired his religious tracts:

> "It is true, the Christian Religion is the most mild and gentle Institution in the whole World, and the fullest of Mercy towards Sinners; but not to insolent and obstinate Sinners, but to the Humble and Penitent. The Gospel itself is Thunder to the impudent and impenitent Transgressors, and the Lamb of God then shows himself the Lion of Judah."

The work he wrote for soldiers — with a dedication to the Duke of Marlborough — was called *The Soldier's Monitor,* and fifteen thousand five hundred copies of it were distributed to soldiers in 1704 and 1705. There was a 30th edition of this 72-page book in 1802. "If a Soldier Steals, Lies, or Swears profanely," wrote Dr. Woodward; "if he drinks to Excess, or does Violence to Man or Woman, he degrades himself and forfeits the honour due to his Station." Similar sentiments were expressed in *The Sailors Monitor,* which according to the records the Society thanked Dr. Woodward for writing in 1701, and which reached a 21st edition in 1818. Other tracts written by him included *The Young Man's Monitor; Kind Caution to Swearers; Baseness of Slandering and Backbiting; Dissuasive from Gaming; Dissuasive from Drunkenness; A Present for Servants; Rebuke to the Sin of Uncleanness;* and *A Kind Caution to Watermen.* There was also a *Short Catechism with an Explanation of Divers Hard Words,* and a farthing tract on the observance of the sabbath. The distribution of tracts was a frequently discussed topic at early meetings of the S.P.C.K., and clearly all these publications were designed to reach as wide a public as possible. Several of Dr. Woodward's titles were reprinted for over one hundred years.

Works by J. F. Osterwald, the Swiss theologian who died in 1747, were also published by the Society over quite a considerable period. The earliest edition I have found of his *An Abridgement of the History of the Bible* is dated 1720, and there was "A New Edition" in 1798. Francis Fox recommended this book to young readers in *An Introduction to Spelling and Reading.*

One of the features of the Society for Promoting Christian Knowledge catalogues is that the cheaper items are usually priced as single copies and also at discount rates for bulk or wholesale purchase. This seems an indication that private individuals could buy at privileged rates in order to distribute the Society's publications free, for while we have evidence that its members arranged for free distribution of tracts amongst various sections of the public, I have found no record that these tracts were carried by hawkers for sale in the usual way as a commercial transaction.

In the catalogue for 1745 there are one hundred and seventeen titles altogether; over thirty items are priced at a penny each or less, and only eighteen of them cost more than 3d. each. Osterwald's *History of the Abridgement of the Bible*, for example, cost ¾d. a copy or 5s. per hundred — a price, incidentally, which had risen by the end of the century of 1½d. or 10s. per hundred. *Pastoral Advice after Confirmation* cost 1d. or 6s. per hundred and Woodward's *Kind Caution to Profane Swearers* cost ½d. or 4s. per hundred. *The Publick House-keeper's Monitor* cost 1½d. or 10s. for 100 copies.

What is striking about the later eighteenth century productions of the Society for Promoting Christian Knowledge is the number of editions that some of them had gone through. Robert Nelson's *Instructions for Them that Come to be Confirmed* had reached a 36th edition in 1798 (it was 2d. a copy or 12s. per hundred); and the same author's *The Sacrament Of The Lord's Supper Explained to the Meanest Capacity* (4d. or 28s. a hundred) was available in a 19th edition in 1799. There was also, in 1800, "A New Edition, Corrected" of *The Church Catechism Broken into Short Questions . . . together with prayers for the use of charity schools,* which contained on page 24 "An Explanation of Some Words in the Church Catechism, for the easier Understanding thereof":

> "Almighty     ... able to do things
> , Descended    ... went down
> Neighbour    ... every Body
> Quick          ... Living, those that shall be found alive upon the Earth at the Day of Judgment
> Repentance   ... Sorrow for Sin, accompanied with a change of Mind and Life."

This kind of explanation illustrated the dictum of another S.P.C.K. tract author that "Children never learn anything with pleasure, which they do not understand."

The good sense of many writers for the Society is not in doubt, neither is their seriousness of purpose in attempting to provide cheap, wholesome religious literature for the poor. Yet when the contents of the twelve-volume "Collected Edition" (1800) of tracts are examined, it is hard to imagine that these could ever have competed with chapbooks in popular appeal.

Methodists, as has been indicated, entered the field of popular publishing comparatively late, and although Wesley himself was a prolific writer and editor, and his publications, including works prepared in collaboration with his brother Charles, numbered three hundred and seventy-one, the Methodist achievement in providing cheap books for the poor is very much more difficult to evaluate than a cursory examination would suggest.

Wesley was a best-selling author, but it is doubtful whether the most popular of his books were either designed for the poor, or indeed reached them in significant numbers. The sources for a study of his authorship are fourfold: firstly, there is G. Osborn's pioneer study, *Outlines of Wesleyan Bibliography* (London, 1869); then there is R. Green's *The Works of John and Charles Wesley* (London, 1896); *The Book Room,* by Frank Cumbers (London, 1956) provides a useful account of Methodist publishing; and finally there are the collections of pamphlets written by Wesley in the Methodist archives, City Road, London, and in the British Museum collection. So far as these publications are concerned we are once again faced with the intractable problem of the survival of ephemeral material, and the bibliographies mentioned must be used to fill in the gaps where no copies are readily available for study and comparison.

Amongst Wesley's most popular titles was *A Collection of Prayers and Hymns,* London, 1741, which was frequently reprinted – an 18th edition appeared in 1825. *The Character of a Methodist* was first published at Bristol in 1742, and a 16th edition came out in 1814. Another widely circulated title was *Hymns for Those that Seek and Those that Have,* London, 1747, 10th edition 1779. Amongst shorter works which were often reprinted were *Instructions for Children,* London, 1745, and *Advice to People Called Methodists,* London, 1745.

One of the cheapest of these books was *Instructions for Children,* which cost 3d. per copy or 20s. per hundred. On the other hand, *A Collection of Psalms and Hymns,* London, 1741, cost 1s., while *Hymns for Those that Seek and Those that Have* was priced at 6d. A catalogue issued in 1756 contained 181 titles, over a quarter of them costing 1d. each; yet the evidence over the period of the century indicates that the Methodists did not seriously rival the established church in the provision of cheap evangelical literature on a really large scale. In *The Wesleyan Movement in the Industrial Revolution*, W. J. Warner comments in terms which remain broadly true of intent if not of achievement:

> "The most completely organised form of educative activity which the movement undertook was the wide dissemination of literature as a project of popular instruction. The early years of the century had already witnessed a striking extension in the publication of inexpensive pamphlets which in some cases achieved an enormous circulation. Wesleyanism adopted the medium as an organised method. Wesley himself was its driving force and the campaign was conducted through a central office, called the Book Room."

The institution of the Book Room dates from 1741, and by 1753 its activities had so increased that Wesley appointed Thomas Butts and William Briggs to run it as Book Stewards. The increasing scope of Methodist publishing is indicated by the fact that in 1795 its receipts were £6598. 4. 9., and the output of the Book Room was extremely varied, as W. J. Warner indicates:

> "It included biography, poetry, travel, subjects of daily utility, etiquette, school books, Christian casuistry, the writings of Locke, Spencer, Shakespeare and Malebranche, as well as explicitly stated religious works."

Our purpose here is simply to trace the extent to which Methodism attempted to provide cheap books for the poor, and it is probable that the greater part of its output was quite unsuitable for them, and often in any case too expensive. It is, moreover, extremely doubtful whether the evangelical excesses which were so often apparent in Methodist writing would have made much appeal to the working class reader for whom taverns, fairs and dances provided the means by which a life of grinding poverty could be made tolerable. What would a working man have made of this kind of confession? It is that of a sailor who in his youth -

> ". . . went to horse-races, wakes, dances, fairs, attended the play-house, nay had so far forgotten the fear of his Maker and the counsel of his mother, that he several times got intoxicated with liquor."

The morbid nature of a good deal of Methodist autobiographical writing is exemplified in John Nelson's autobiography, first published in 1767:

> ". . . When I was between nine and ten years old, I was horribly terrified with the thoughts of death and judgement whenever I was alone."

The appeal of this kind of writing to those outside Methodist circles must have been extremely limited, and the introspection which Methodism encouraged bred such hysterical outbreaks as the emotional revival at Kingswood School in 1768 described by A. H. Body in *John Wesley and*

*Education,* London, 1936. A good deal of early religious instruction amongst Wesley's followers conveyed the message that fear — synonymous with terror — were necessary steps to communion with God.

One of Wesley's books, however, was free from overtones of introspection and confession. This was *Primitive Physic,* which was first published in 1747 and had reached a 23rd edition before its author died in 1791. Of all Wesley's books this "home doctor" was the one which most clearly anticipated the cheap non-fiction publishing of the nineteenth and twentieth centuries, and in his own day it must have been a very useful handbook. Certainly it was extremely popular, but again we must ask whether in fact it was designed for the poorer reader — probably not, for its price of one shilling would have effectively prevented their purchasing it.

Towards the end of the century, in 1782, John Wesley made a very real effort to cater for the very poorest reader. In this year he issued a broadsheet entitled *A Plan of the Society Instituted in January, 1782, to Distribute Religious Tracts among the Poor*[1]. "I cannot", wrote Wesley upon this sheet, "but earnestly recommend this, to all those who desire to see true scriptural Christianity spread throughout these nations. Men wholly unawakened will not take the pains to read the Bible. They have no relish for it. But a small Tract may engage their attention for Half an hour: and may, by the blessing of God, prepare them for going forward."

The scheme was that members were to pay an annual subscription of half a guinea or more, and according to the subscriptions so tracts would be received for distribution. Subscribers were permitted to choose the tracts they wanted from a list of thirty, the most expensive of which was an 8d. edition of John Law's *A Serious Call to a Holy Life.* Other titles cost as little as 3s. per hundred, and some were cheaper, costing 1s. 6d. or 1s. per hundred. So far as I know none of these tracts has survived, but it does seem from the extremely

1. There is an apparently unique copy of this broadsheet in the Methodist Archives, City Road, London. I am grateful to the Archivist, The Rev. J. Bowmer, for having drawn my attention to it.

low price of some of them that they can have consisted of only a single sheet, or at the most a few pages, and they were clearly intended to be distributed to the poor by subscribers to the Society.

An earlier venture of Wesley's may have been a factor in his decision to found a tract society. One of his works, *An Extract of the Life and Death of Mr. John Janeway,* had been published in London in 1753. Some years later it was reprinted in a 1½d. edition, and in 1775 another edition appeared with the words "not to be sold, but given away" printed upon it. Another circumstance which probably influenced Wesley was the sheer volume of the S.P.C.K.'s publishing programme. At all events, the tract enterprise struck deep roots within the Methodist movement, and in 1810 we find J. Crowther urging that books and other publications should be disseminated by hawkers, and that such a practice would not cause the Book Room to suffer financially. This was *An Apology for the Liberty of the Press Among the Methodists,* a forthright pamphlet examining the attempt to prevent preachers from publishing on their own account and an investigation of book hawkers.

A striking feature of the Methodist tract movement is that the theory of tract production and distribution was derived from practice – a splendid example of Methodist empiricism! The principles laid down in the early nineteenth century had been anticipated in the practice both of the Methodists and of the Society for Promoting Christian Knowledge during the previous century. It was in fact in 1822 that the Methodist Conference in London began to concern itself with the problem, and asked "What is the judgement of the Conference relative to the circulation of Religious Tracts?". The answer makes clear that the matter was being successfully carried on without the direction of the Conference:

"We have heard with much satisfaction of the successful exertions of our Societies in various parts of the Kingdom, in distributing Religious Tracts especially amongst those who are either destitute of the ordinary means of

Scriptural Instruction, or neglect to improve those means
. . .''

It was proposed that a General Tract Committee should be
set up, consisting of the President and the Secretary (i.e. of
Conference) together with "Preachers" and "Gentlemen"
from town and country. Criteria were laid down for the
tracts; above all they were to be both interesting and
doctrinally correct; there was to be a variety of titles, and
prices were to be kept as low as possible; good stocks of titles
were to be maintained; and all new tracts were to be
approved by a sub-committee. [2]

Typical of the kind of publication with which the
Committee concerned itself was *An Address to Persons who
Complain they have No Time to Prepare for Eternity: with an
interesting account of a galley slave*, London, 1810. This
tract had eight pages, and was unillustrated, while its extremely
dull subject matter was badly printed. On page 8 there was a
list of twenty-three other tracts at prices ranging from 6d. to
1d.

The Methodists followed up the establishment of their
Tract Committee with a pamphlet which appeared in about
1830 entitled *An Address on Religious Tract Distribution with
a Word to the Distributors*. It was issued anonymously, at a
price of 3s. per hundred copies; and the author may well have
been John Mason, Book Steward from 1827 to 1864, who
published an extremely large number of tracts, many of them
with illustrations, at prices which varied – 2s. per hundred
for 8-page tracts, 3s. per hundred for 12-page tracts, and 4s.
per hundred for 16-page tracts.

Once more we see that the comments made upon this kind
of publishing could so easily belong to the preceding century:

2. There were numerous tract societies in the early years of the
nineteenth century. They followed the establishment of the
Religious Tract Society in 1799, and have never been investigated.
They are mainly of interest for the somewhat oblique light they
throw upon the state of literacy amongst the poor. See the following
chapter.

"It is a cheap and easy method of diffusing saving knowledge, especially amongst young people, and the poorer classes of society."

It is further urged that tracts should be short, so that they can be soon read and easily remembered. This "suits mechanics and labourers who have neither inclination nor time for volumes". Travellers should give them to innkeepers, waiters, coachmen, fellow-travellers, and to others met upon journeys. Besides supplying those who have been taught to read with wholesome material, tracts are regarded as an antidote to "a flood of infidel and licentious publications . . . written in a popular style . . . seasoned with a vulgar wit."

Finally, there is a brief history of Wesleyan tracts with instructions upon forming a tract society, and the booklet ends with an exhortation to tract distributors, who must be punctual, persevering, zealous, prayerful, consistent.

The clue to an evaluation of popular evangelical literature is to be found, paradoxically, in the nature of the chapbook. This was essentially escapist and offered, perhaps upon a superficial level, a retreat into the world of imagination far removed from the daily toil which was the lot of the eighteenth century poor. The religious tract, on the other hand, bleakly counselled acceptance of conditions, however harsh, and pointed out unceasingly that the underprivileged members of society ought to be content with lives of unremitting labour, while holding fast to their Christian faith. I have found no reference amongst the scanty autobiographical literature of the time to the reading of a tract or any impression which this made; and certainly, by their very lack of imaginative content, tracts must have failed to provide any stimulus for the inner life of eighteenth century labouring men and women. This was the basic defect of evangelical popular literature. At a time when society was changing, well-intentioned men of religion provided a large number of cheap publications which were almost entirely hortatory, and neglected the popular imagination which had been nourished in a pre-literate society by oral culture and the communal ceremonies and customs connected with the agrarian cycle of the year.[3]

Because tracts failed to satisfy such needs, and were in any case extremely dull, men and women who had been taught to read and who were living in a society where the printed word was playing an increasingly important part, turned to chapbooks. These provided not only a link with the past, but also a means of moving into a literate society which was becoming dominated to an ever-growing extent by industrialism, with the consequent need for labouring men to assert their new identity as members of the working class.

3. No comprehensive work on this important subject has yet been written. See J. Brand, *Observations on the Popular Antiquities of Great Britain*, 3 Vols. (Bohn Edition), London, 1849; also T. F. Thiselton Dyer, *British Popular Customs*, London, 1876. A number of nineteenth century antiquaries gathered a great deal of material on this topic which has yet to be analysed. Perhaps the most valuable study to date is Ruth A. Firor's *Folkways in Thomas Hardy*, Pennsylvania, 1931, Reprint New York, 1962.

# Chapter 7

## CONCLUSION

It is primarily within the political frame of reference, touched upon briefly at the end of the preceding chapter, that we must seek evidence for the existence of a mass reading public round about eighteen hundred. But before doing so, it may be convenient to retrace in outline the argument so far, and then to draw specific conclusions about the development of chapbook printing in the eighteenth century.

We have followed the discussion of educational theory so far as it affected the provision of elementary instruction for the poor. The views of those who favoured it and those who opposed it were rooted in an identical desire to preserve the rigid class structure of society intact. We have seen the way in which attempts to provide schooling for poor children worked out in practice, and examined the way in which reading was taught. Finally, we have looked in some detail at the cheap publications – both secular and religious – which were designed for working men and women to read. Our discussion of this extremely important topic centred upon chapbooks, and from the reconstruction of the chapbook trade in Appendix (ii), several points emerge.

In the first place it must be emphasised that the Dicey family, who were in business for about 75 years, were the most important publishers of chapbooks; and their ascendancy underlines the pre-eminence of London as the centre of printing and book production.

From the details given it is apparent that from the last two decades of the previous century until William Dicey began printing in the seventeen twenties, there had been a quite surprisingly large number of individual printers who, so far as the records can now show, included a few chapbook titles in their productions of broadside ballads and books on a variety of subjects. Amongst these earlier printers T. Norris is one whose output of chapbooks seems to have been quite considerable – and Thomas Gent has recorded that Norris became "a very rich bookseller".

It was the Diceys who recognised the growing opportunities in this field, and made a speciality of printing chapbooks. Clearly this enterprise proved successful: they acquired additional premises, their trade expanded, and successive generations of Diceys gave every evidence that the firm had prospered.

By mid-century the evidence shows many instances of active co-operation between printers, and this suggests strongly that the chapbook trade was becoming increasingly profitable. In 1760 Woodgate and Brooks were advertising at one time 150 different titles; and Hodges – who again collaborated with several other individual printers in the production of many chapbooks, besides more substantial works – certainly became an outstandingly successful man.

Towards the end of the century we see the trend for the chapbook trade to be almost entirely in the hands of specialists, larger family concerns who followed, and indeed challenged, the example set by the Dicey family. There was "The London & Middlesex Printing Office" run by the Sabines; there was the Sympson family who ran "Sympson's Warehouse"; and one member of the Marshall family in 1764 listed 150 chapbook titles. From this latter part of the century, too, catalogues and lists issued by Larkin How suggest a very considerable output, although few of his chapbooks have survived.

Equally significant, of course, was the spread of printing in the provincial towns of England. In Newcastle, chapbooks were printed as early as 1711, and at York in 1724, while Birmingham was another town where they were being produced early in the century. These were all important centres of the chapbook trade; and after 1760, ephemeral popular literature was being produced in considerable quantities in Banbury, Nottingham, Coventry and Manchester. Less important towns, from the point of view of such printing, were Sheffield – where there was a printer in 1736 – Worcester, Tewkesbury and Leicester where printers were at work in about 1760. During the last forty years of the century some chapbooks were being printed in Carlisle, Durham, Whitehaven and Stockton.

In both London and the provinces, then, we see a steady increase in chapbook production, and it seems reasonable to conclude from this that there was a steady rise in the number of readers. It is difficult to measure the growth in literacy during the eighteenth century, or indeed at any period, but almost certainly it was a gradual development. In support of this view there seems to be only one example of a revolution in language planning with regard to mass literacy, and this occurred in Turkey in 1928 when the Arabic alphabet was replaced by a modified Latin script which became law in November of the same year. A "School of the Nation" was founded, with Ataturk himself as chief instructor, and within a year more than one million citizens had received its diploma in reading and writing.

I can find no other example of a leap into mass literacy of this kind, and it appears in general that the growth of reading ability is a gradual affair. In England the increase in readership amongst the poor seems to have taken place without what G. H. Bantock has called a "psychic dislocation" amongst the working classes who during the eighteenth century were coming into close contact with a print culture for the first time. The smoothness of the transition from a non-literate to a literate society in this country is due mainly to the fact that most of the material available for the poor to read was of a traditional nature, and had formed part of the oral background of story and song which began to find its way into print, in a form designed for mass circulation, towards the end of the seventeenth century.

It was not, however, until a century later that the existence of a reading public amongst the poor was fully realised. The individual working man, subjected to the pressures of industrialism, had become a member of the emergent working class with a group consciousness and an identity of interest which was eventually to reorder society in a decisive fashion. An American historian, W. Bowden, has described in *Industrial Society in England Towards the End of the Eighteenth Century,* the process by which this happened:

" . . . As for the industrial workers, they were being concentrated in cities and economically homogeneous groups. They were subjected to a common administrative discipline. They were reduced to a common level of wages and working conditions – a common level which contrasted with the entirely different plane of income and of living conditions on which the employing group lived . . . . In respect alike to his work, to his living conditions, and to the promotion of his welfare, the individual worker was more and more merged in the group. The group concept was literally thrust upon him."

As we shall see, the fact that by the end of the century popular reading was possible on a more serious note helped the individual worker's awareness of this group concept.

The implications for society of the growth of the working class are not part of the present enquiry, except in one respect. How did it throw the question of mass literacy into relief, against a background of social change; and as a corollary to this, what was the significance of literacy to the working class?

In beginning to answer the first of these questions, we find that in 1791-2, Thomas Paine published the two parts of his *Rights of Man;* and in the controversy which followed, he issued in 1792 a pamphlet, *A Letter Addressed to the Addressers of the Late Proclamation,* in which he made an important reference to a cheap edition of his book:

"The original edition of the first and second parts of "Rights of Man" having been expensively printed (in the modern style of printing pamphlets, that they might be bound up with Mr. Burke's Reflections on the French Revolution), the high price precluded the generality of people from purchasing, and many applications were made to me from various parts of the country to print the work in a cheaper manner. The people of Sheffield requested leave to print two thousand copies for themselves, with which request I immediately complied. The same request came to me from Rotherham, from Leicester, from Chester, from several towns in Scotland; and Mr. James Mackintosh, author of "Vindiciae Gallicae", brought me a request from Warwickshire for leave to print ten thousand copies in that county. I had already sent a cheap edition to Scotland; and finding the applications increase, I concluded that the best method of complying therewith would be to print a very numerous edition in London, under my own direction, by which means the work would be more perfect, and the price reduced lower than it could be by printing small editions in the country of only a few thousand each."

The interest of this passage lies mainly in the fact that the existence of a considerable public who would purchase and read a *cheap* edition of *Rights of Man* is assumed by its author without question, and also that such a cheap edition is being prepared in response to a definite demand from this public. Even if due allowance is made for the propensity of a writer to overestimate the demand for his own work, this quotation from Paine illuminates and extends a comment attributed to Burke that at this period there were eighty thousand readers in England.

An assumption that the ability to read is vital if radical ideas are to be disseminated appears to be implicit in Paine's response to these requests for cheap reprints of this particular work. To complement this view of literacy as an element in political agitation, we must see how the ability to read was regarded by those who had no wish to encourage political discussion amongst the working class, and who wished to preserve the status quo.

The influence of the French Revolution was evident in radical circles. In 1794, for example, the Corresponding Society – a radical organisation – at its annual dinner toasted "The Armies contending for Liberty", or in other words the Republican army that was at war with England, and the band played the "Marseillaise". As G. D. H. Cole expressed it, "The first attempts of the workers at independent political organisation rose directly out of the events in France; the speed and severity with which they were crushed was directly due to the fear which those events had inspired".

At the same time these events, and the subsequent threat of invasion by Napoleon, provided the opportunity for an appeal to be made to the patriotism of all Englishmen to resist the invader – and in this, literacy played its part. In many cases the appeal was a thinly disguised exhortation to working men to accept their conditions of work and not be influenced by the revolutionary events which had taken place across the Channel. Whether the reminder that a "unanimous defiance of the common enemy" was required, or whether this assumption of the unity of interest amongst all Englishmen was taken seriously by working men, it is impossible to tell; but the seriousness with which the appeal was put forward cannot be doubted. An 8-page pamphlet entitled *Popular and Patriotic Tracts* was published on the 23rd August, 1803, and the first page outlines the thinking which prompted it:

" . . . at the present important period, when the utmost energies of a Free and Independent People, will be necessary to repel the attacks of an Invading and Implacable Enemy, it has been thought requisite to point out, by every means and in every shape, the *situation* in which *we stand,* the *character* of our *ambitious* and *tyrannical enemy;* and what may be *naturally expected* from *his success* on the British shores. With this view, many Gentlemen of intelligence and patriotism have written and published a series of animating and encouraging addresses on the most interesting topics which can at this crisis engage the public mind; together with certain Most Striking and Notorious Facts, illustrative of the character of the enemy; facts, which it would be as absurd to conceal, as it is impossible to refute. The Dissemination of these in the metropolis, and its vicinity, has already produced the happiest effect – Harmony among Ourselves, and an Unanimous Defiance of the Common Enemy.

That the same spirit may be extended to the remotest parts of the Kingdom: the following List of Tracts, with the Booksellers' Names and Prices, is submitted to the nobility, gentry, and clergy; and it is hoped that by contributing to circulate such of them as they may judge proper for their respective tenantry, or parishioners, they may excite an universal sentiment of gratitude for the Civil and Religious Privileges we have long enjoyed, and an active zeal to defend them against Foreign Hostility, or Domestic Innovation."

[The closing phrase "domestic innovation" was an obvious reference to political agitators and reformers.]

I have quoted the introductory material at length because it illustrates so clearly the assumption on the part of the government's supporters that national unity was a sentiment that could be appealed to directly through the medium of the written word — although it is hard to imagine that the Birmingham mob which sacked Dr. Priestley's house in 1794 did so in response to having read pamphlets like those advertised, or that the belligerent drayman who attacked Zachariah Coleman for not raising his hat when the King drove past had one of them in his pocket.[1]

The prices of these tracts ranged from 3d. to ½d. each. There were special prices for bulk purchase, and the desire of authors and publishers to reach the widest possible audience is illustrated by the fact that out of seventy-three titles, only thirteen cost more than one penny. The emphasis is very much upon mass distribution. The most intriguing title in the entire list if *Horrors upon Horrors. A true narrative of the sufferings of a Hanoverian blacksmith, who died raving mad, in consequence of the dreadful scenes of barbarity of which he had been late an eye-witness in his own country.* More usual are *A Shopkeeper's Address to his Fellow Citizens* or a *Song for All True Britons,* sung to the tune of "Rule Britannia".

Again, it must be stressed that it is not the contents of these publications that concern our present enquiry, but the assumptions made by their producers about the existence of a reading public who would be able to cope with the printed word, and be influenced by it.

1. For these two references see H. N. Brailsford, *Shelley, Godwin, and Their Circles,* London, reprinted 1925, Ch. 1, "The French Revolution"; also "Mark Rutherford's" novel *The Revolution in Tanner's Lane* (1887), Ch. 1. Coleman himself is an excellent portrait of the literate, radical working man of the early nineteenth century.

If by now we have established that literacy amongst the poor at the end of the eighteenth century was seen within a political context – and both reformers and those who argued for the status quo saw literacy, by implication at least, as a weapon in the social struggle – we may turn to the other question, posed earlier: what was the significance of literacy to the working class?

An attempt to answer this question involves at the outset a brief mention of the role played by literacy in society. As M. M. Lewis has put it in *The Importance of Illiteracy*:

> "The true importance of literacy today is that it has such close relations with what a modern society does, thinks, and feels. In every society the extent and the standards of literacy are intimately bound up with its ideals and purposes, and with its political, economic, and general social behaviour."

Although written to describe a twentieth century situation, this passage is equally true of the last decade of the eighteenth, with the proviso that the ideals and purposes of working men were connected with the improvement of their lot and the achievement of a working class identity. Earlier in the century, the instinctive response of workers to intolerable conditions or increases in the cost of living had often found expression in violence, but at the close of the period an important new element, the existence of a large reading public, reshaped working class attitudes. The ability to read and the ready availability of Paine's *Rights of Man* meant that communication was possible at a more sophisticated level than that of a demagogue haranguing a mob. To quote Lewis once more, "without communication no politics . . . this means no effective political life without literacy." If then at working class level we have a considerable degree of literacy, then working class politics becomes a reality.

The importance of reading in this process is best illustrated by reference to Richard Carlile and James Watson – both born in the eighteenth century – who were the first publishers to specialise in the large-scale production of cheap propagandist books. They were not, of course, the first radical printers, but the size of their respective output makes them the first specialists in this field. Carlile was born in Ashburton, Devonshire, in 1790, and became a publisher in London in 1817 when he issued *Wat Tyler,* an early poem by Southey that the poet had vainly tried to suppress, and sold twenty-five thousand copies of it. Carlile followed this up with other titles, most notable of which was an edition of Paine's political works. The outspokennesss of Carlile's attacks upon religion brought him into conflict with the law, and he was prosecuted on several occasions.[2] He died, after a life devoted to radical publishing, in 1843.

James Watson was born in 1799, and in 1831 became a printer and publisher. By 1842 he was issuing a 4-page catalogue of books and pamphlets, all of which were in opposition to established political and religious beliefs. He continued in business until 1854, when his stock was bought by G. J. Holyoake who carried on Watson's tradition of radical and freethought publishing. Watson's biographer, W. J. Linton, said of him that he —

" . . . cared rather than for profit to place good reading before the uneducated reader; wherefore he was content with the smallest margin of gain enough for the means of life. But he cared also for the correctness and decent appearance of his books, even the cheapest."

He died in 1874 at Lower Norwood in London.

Further evidence of the ability of working men to read is found in a small book by W. H. Reid, *The Rise and Dissolution of the Infidel Societies in this Metropolis,* London, 1800. It contains a forthright attack upon religious unbelief, and reflects the author's belief that the habit of reading was widespread amongst artizans. Even those "who despised the labour of reading", he claimed, took their opinions from those who could.

The chief object of Reid's disapproval was the reading club where working men would gather in order to discuss religion

2. See G. A. Aldred, *Richard Carlile Agitator His Life and Times,* 3rd Ed., Glasgow, 1941, passim, for an account of Carlile's activities. See also W. H. Wickwar, *The Struggle for the Freedom of the Press, 1819-1832,* London, 1928, for a less partisan account of Carlile.

and politics in a way that could hardly have been acceptable
to holders of more orthodox beliefs. In 1795, for example,
there was such a Reading Society in the club room of the
Green Dragon Inn in Fore Street, near Cripplegate, where
Sunday debates went on until one in the morning. There was
also "The Moral and Revolutionary Society", which met near
Bunhill Row, and published "Revolutionary pamphlets".
There was a hair-dresser's shop in Shoreditch High Street
where theology was debated on Sunday mornings, and there
were branches of this club in Whitechapel, Spitalfields and
Hoxton. At The Angel in Cecil Court, St. Martin's Lane,
there was a club which met on Sundays and Wednesdays until
February, 1798.

The clubs are summed up in the following manner:

> "Next to songs, in which the clergy were a standing subject
> of abuse; in conjunction with pipes and tobacco, the tables
> of the club-rooms were frequently strewed with penny,
> two-penny, and three-penny publications, as it were so
> many swivels against established opinions; while to enable
> the members to furnish themselves with the heavy artillery
> of Voltaire, Godwin, etc., reading-clubs were formed."

Whether these clubs were regarded as breeding grounds for
disaffection in politics and religion, or were taken to be
notable examples of self-help in adult education, depended
very much upon one's view of society. W. H. Reid clearly saw
them in the former light. William Lovett, the Chartist, on the
other hand, had no doubts about the value of such
gatherings, and in an unpublished letter to Francis Place
dated the 17th November, 1834, he described his own
attendance at one of them:

> "Sir about twelve years ago, chance introduced me into a
> little society composed of intelligent, and chiefly young
> men, who held their meetings at a house in the vicinity of
> Leicester Fields. They by a trifling weekly subscription
> had accumulated a Library of the most choice and to me
> valuable books; as I was very superstitious, and entirely
> ignorant on the subjects of society, politics, the arts,
> sciences, indeed on most subjects of which I have since

acquired some *little* knowledge. By their conversations and discussions together with the books I read I acquired a taste for mixing with companions of their description; and ever since that society has been broken up I have sought after, and been in the habit of meeting once or twice a week with persons who have acquired a similar taste."

Such reading clubs as Lovett describes are evidence of the interest taken by some working men at least in serious problems, and of their ability to read. In his autobiography, Lovett speaks of a more general interest in books when describing a venture in co-operative retailing in 1828:

"The members of those societies (i.e. Co-operative Trading Association) subscribed a small weekly sum for the raising of a common fund, with which they opened a general store, containing such articles of food, clothing, books, etc., as were most in request among working men."

Less seriously minded readers than those to whom Lovett was referring were catered for by James Catnach, who had begun in business as a printer of street ballads and children's books at the Seven Dials in London in 1813. His most sensational productions were single sheets giving details of the most gruesome murders of the day, the sales of which were often quite phenomenal. It is said, for example, that he sold over one and a half million copies of his sheet on the celebrated Maria Marten and the Red Barn murder case, and two and a half million each of his publications on the Rush and the Manning cases, revolting murders which caught the popular imagination. These sheets were sold to itinerant salesmen known as "patterers" at 3d. per dozen! – and at this period newspapers were very much more expensive.

Another effort to reach a wide public was made by the Yorkshire printer and publisher, William Milner, whose "Cottage Library" cost only 6d. or 1s. per title and included a number of classics of English Literature as well as titles like "Why Did He Marry Her?" or "Righted at Last". William Milner was the first publisher to provide not only established works of literature but also popular fiction in a cheap and durable form. When he died in 1850, the business he had founded was continued by relatives, and was still in existence in 1897.

Other printers were active, though upon a smaller scale, in similar enterprises. We are, however, moving out of the chronological period which is the subject of this study; and before drawing to a close, there is one other pointer to the extent of literacy which must be considered. This was the publication in 1832 of the first number of *The Penny Magazine,* sponsored by the Society for the Diffusion of Useful Knowledge. Charles Knight, the Editor and Publisher, went out of his way in the first number to stress that he hoped the magazine would "tend to fix the mind upon calmer, and, it may be, purer subjects of thought than the violence of party discussion, or the stimulating details of crime and suffering."

Some thirteen years earlier Knight had written in *The Windsor Express* of "the excessive spread of cheap publications almost exclusively directed to the united object of inspiring hatred of the Government and contempt of the Religious Institutions of the country." It is clear that this was still his attitude when he edited *The Penny Magazine;* and the failure of the journal to discuss politics was the reason, according to a contemporary observer, for its failure to circulate as widely as it might have done amongst factory operatives. The most interesting fact about this enterprise is that soon after its appearance it was selling 200,000 copies in weekly numbers and monthly parts, and although its sale had dropped to 40,000 in the mid-forties, the earlier figure represents a very considerable reading public in existence in 1832. Knight indeed calculated that soon after its inception the magazine had one million readers, and if we take this fact together with that of Catnach's *sale* of over two million copies of a sensational sheet, it is safe to assume that by 1832 a mass reading public was in existence.

In tracing the extent of such literacy, we have travelled, inevitably, a long way from the eighteenth century school-room and the chapbooks of London Bridge or Bow Churchyard. What I have attempted to show is that the considerable amount of literacy amongst working men and women at the beginning of the nineteenth century was no sudden phenomenon, but rather the outcome of a steady increase in the number of readers amongst the poor in eighteenth century England.

In one important respect, however, the situation at the outset of the nineteenth century was different: literacy had come to be regarded by many as a weapon in the social and political struggles in which the working class found themselves to an ever-increasing extent involved. This fact gave an ironic twist to earlier arguments as to whether the poor should receive elementary instruction or not. Those who had favoured teaching them to read on the grounds that they would thereby remain pious and content with their humble role in society, were proved wrong. Men who had opposed such basic education had done so mainly because they sensed the power implicit in being able to read; and in this belief they were absolutely right. Working class literacy, which made working class politics possible, proved to be a potent weapon which had been forged, almost unknowingly, throughout the eighteenth century, in class-rooms where poor children learned to read, and in the printing offices of men like Cluer Dicey.

# APPENDICES

Teachers at the Charity School in Soho, London (taken from J. H. Cardwell, *The Story of a Charity School,* London, 1899, p. 32 ff. & p. 66 ff.)

For both male and female teachers the year of appointment and the annual salary is quoted. Rooms were provided in every case.

## MALE TEACHERS

| 1699 | Mr. Walsh | £30 |
| 1700 | Mr. Macbeth | £30 |
| 1701 | Mr. Gray | £30 |
| 1702 | Mr. Ford | £30 |
| 1712 | Mr. Reed | £30 |
| 1716 | Mr. Shanks | £32 |
| 1736 | Mr. Harris | £36 |

(£4 of this sum was an extra payment for teaching girls to write).

1762 Mr. Sanger £34
(After nine years, he retired on a pension of £14 p.a. He was 48 when he was appointed, and drew his pension for four years).

1771 Mr. Blake £26
(£6 p.a. was deducted from his salary in order to help towards paying the pension of his predecessor. In 1788 he received 2 guineas extra payment "in consideration of the increased price of sope, chips etc.". He resigned in 1790 and was presented with 20 guineas).

1790 Mr. Thompson £36
(He was elected by ballot, and was dismissed in 1792 for

## FEMALE TEACHERS

| 1704 | Mrs. Moor | £26 |
| 1726 | Mrs. Shanks | £20 |
| 1735 | Mrs. Collins | £26 |
| 1741 | Mrs. Walker | £26 |

(She died one month after her appointment on probation, following the death of Mrs. Collins. Mrs. Walker had petitioned the board to be appointed).

| 1741 | Mrs. Salmon | £26 |
| 1741 | Mrs. Naseby | £26 |
| 1742 | Mrs. Hubble | £26 |
| 1758 | Mrs. Hughes | £26 |
| 1762 | Mrs. Whetton | £26 |
| 1762 | Mrs. Lewis | £26 |
| 1763 | Mrs. Jackson | £26 |
| 1773 | Mrs. Hamp | £26 |
| 1784 | Mrs. Hatton | £26 |

(In addition to rooms, Mrs. Hatton received "Coal and Candles". She had been chosen by ballot from 42 candidates).

1784 Mrs. Hough £26
(With "Coal and Candles". She was chosen by ballot from 54 candidates).

making children purchase from
him "useless books, pictures,
etc.").
1792 Mr. Thomas          £34
(Besides accommodation, he
received "other advantages", but
these are not specified).
1798 Mr. J. Sturla    About £65
(The rise in salary is explained
by the admission to the school
of "pay" children. He resigned
on the 8th March, 1800).

## APPENDIX (ii)

## INTRODUCTION

The chapbook trade, at first sight, presents a picture of extreme
confusion. Not only was the distinction between printer, publisher
and bookseller blurred and often non-existent, but the chapbooks
themselves offer a bewildering variety of title pages, almost always
undated, and sometimes with no imprint at all. A large number of
chapbooks were simply "Licensed and Entered According to Order",
"Printed in this Present Year", or "Printed and Sold in London".
Many give no indication at all of where or by whom they were
printed. In the virtual absence of any surviving records of those who
were engaged in the trade, the chapbooks themselves offer the most
important evidence from which a picture of eighteenth century chapbook printing may be reconstructed.

Fortunately a considerable number has survived, and they are
readily available for study. In Great Britain there are important and
extensive collections in the British Museum, the Bodleian Library, the
National Library of Scotland, and St. Bride's Institute; moreover
there are libraries in provincial cities which have holdings of locally
printed chapbooks. In the public library at Newcastle upon Tyne
there are John Bell's "Collections" towards a history of the Newcastle Press. Two manuscript versions (one incomplete) of Frederick
Leary's (unpublished) "The History of the Manchester Periodical
Press" form part of the collection of Manchester Reference Library.
Such sources often augment the information which can be gleaned
from chapbooks themselves. None of the material mentioned above
has been individually catalogued. In the United States, however, large
numbers of chapbooks are to be found in the Harvard College
Library and in New York Public Library, and these have been listed
in detail: the catalogues, with their careful descriptions and lists of
printers, are a valuable source of information — more particularly so
since most of the entries in them relate to English material.

One other source is the catalogue of J. O. Halliwell's collection.
Although the items in it have long since been dispersed, the catalogue

of 240 chapbooks (there are in fact 241 entries; No. 152 is an Elizabethan Horn-book) is of especial interest on account of the notes provided by Halliwell. These reflect the compiler's deep knowledge of English popular literature, and his belief that a study of it would shed much light upon customs, manners and attitudes of the past.

From an educational point of view, the large number of chapbooks which were published indicates that a considerable number of poor people were able to read; but a greater significance is to be attached to the *increase* in the number of chapbooks.

The supply of cheap books in the eighteenth century was very much greater than has been supposed, and the steady increase in their numbers throughout this period provides the most important clue we possess to the efficacy of attempts to educate the poor, and to the spread of literacy amongst them.

The year 1693 is a crucial one, for it was then that restrictions upon printers were lifted, and the way was clear for printing to develop in the provincial towns of England and Wales. In spite of the increase in the number of printers who set up their presses outside London, the capital remained the centre of the book trade.

The following account of printers, publishers and booksellers in England is divided into two sections, London and the Provinces; and it is designed to indicate the extent of the trade and to illustrate its increase during the period in question.

## BIBLIOGRAPHICAL NOTE.

Most of the information presented here has been gleaned from a study of individual chapbooks and publishers' catalogues. Another source has been the work of H. R. Plomer, whose dictionaries, while not containing details of all chapbook printers, are invaluable. The works in question are:

1. H. R. Plomer, *A Dictionary of the Printers and Booksellers Who were at Work in England, Scotland and Ireland from 1668 to 1725,* The Bibliographical Society, 1922.
2. H. R. Plomer, *A Dictionary of the Printers and Booksellers Who were at Work in England, Scotland and Ireland from 1726 to 1775,* The Bibliographical Society, 1932.

There are also:

3. J. L. Crawford (26th Earl of), *Bibliotheca Lindesiana: Catalogue of a Collection of English Ballads of the 17th and 18th Centuries,* 2 Vols., 1890 (Reprint 1962). There is a list of printers, some of whom issued chapbooks.
4. Arundell Esdaile, *A List of English Tales and Prose Romances Printed Before 1740,* The Bibliographical Society, 1912.
5. C. H. Timperley, *A Dictionary of Printers and Printing,* London, 1839.

## A NOTE ON LOCATIONS

The most important centres of chapbook production in London were:

LONDON BRIDGE.

See especially:

    (i) An Antiquary, *Chronicles of London Bridge,* 2nd Ed., London, 1839, pp. 275–278

    (ii) G. Home, *Old London Bridge,* London, 1931, pp. 223–226.

    (iii) H. R. Plomer, *The Booksellers of London Bridge.*

    (iv) H. R. Plomer, *The Church of St. Magnus and the Booksellers of London Bridge.*

BOW CHURCHYARD.

Situated to the South of Cheapside, on the West side of St. Mary le Bow, in Cordwainer Ward.

See H. A. Harben, *A Dictionary of London.*

Bow Churchyard was the address of the Dicey family for many years.

LITTLE BRITAIN.

Situated West out of Aldersgate Street and North to Smithfield, in Aldersgate Ward and Farringdon Ward Without.

See J. T. Smith, *The Streets of London,* New Edition, London, 1854, p. 329. See also H. A. Harben, op. cit.

PYE CORNER.

At the Northern end of Giltspur Street, leading to West Smithfield, in Farringdon Ward Without.

See H. A. Harben, op. cit.

The following description of Pye Corner is from a scarce children's book, *City Scenes, or a Peep into London,* London, 1828:

"3. Pie Corner.

West Smithfield, where you see the white projecting house, as it was left after the fire of London, which took place at midnight, 2nd September, 1666, and burnt with unbated fury till the 10th of the same month. There is also, at the corner of the lane, against a public house called The Fortune of War, a figure of a boy carved in wood, on which was painted an inscription to commemorate the event, and also stating the calamity to have been a punishment on the city for the sin of gluttony; but this being since considered a vulgar error, it is not painted on the new figure, which in other respects is exactly like the old figure first put up".

PRINTERS, PUBLISHERS AND BOOKSELLERS IN LONDON.

[In alphabetical order.]

BALLARD, Samuel.

One of Ballard's imprints was: "Printed and Sold for Samuel

Ballard at the Blue Ball in Little Britain"; and he was apparently in business for a number of years from the beginning of the century. *The Lives and Amours of the Empresses, etc.*, 1723, has on the title page "Sold by S. Ballard."

BATES Charles.
S.
E.

Bates finished his apprenticeship in 1690, and was trained as a ballad printer. One of his early chapbooks, *Guy of Warwick*, circa 1700, is in the Harvard Collection (see also Foster, J.). A 4th Edition of *A New Academy of Compliments* was printed for C. Bates in Giltspur Street and A. Bettesworth on London Bridge, 1715. In 1728 *The New History of the Trojan Wars* was "printed for C. Bates". His address was The Sun and Bible in Pye Corner. Besides broadside ballads and chapbooks, Bates published other books — for example *The Adventures of Five Englishmen, etc.* by Walter Vaughan, ND (1714); but his output of ephemeral literature was considerable and probably represented his chief interest. S. Bates was almost certainly Sara, his wife, who was in business in 1720 when she published a chapbook edition of Forde's *Montelion* in collaboration with A. Bettesworth, C. Hitch, J. Osborn, S. Birt and J. Hodges. An undated chapbook, *The Strange and Wonderful History and Prophecies of Mother Shipton*, in New York Public Library, was "Printed for E. Bates at the Star and Bible in Gilt-spur Street". Perhaps he was a son of C. Bates.

BETTESWORTH, A.

A bookseller at the Red Lion on London Bridge. An edition of *Guy of Warwick* printed by William Onley (q.v.) for E. B. (E. Blare) in 1706 was "sold by A. Bettesworth". He was also associated with S. Bates (q.v.) and G. Hitch (q.v.); and in 1715 he and C. Bates brought out a 4th Edition of *A New Academy of Compliments*. His will was proved in 1739.

BEW, J.

"A Catalogue of Chapmen's books, printed for and sold by J. Bew at No. 28 Paternoster Row" is found at the end of an edition of *Guy of Warwick* printed for Stanley Crowder (Harvard Catalogue 485, p. 29). Bew also published an edition of *Fair Rosamond* in 1789. He was in business by about 1774, and he specialised in ephemeral and popular literature.

BIRT, S.

See Bates, S.

BLAND, T.

An undated chapbook, *Here is a Full and True Relation of one Mr. Rich Langly, a Glazier*, was "Printed for T. Bland near Fleet Street". An F. Bland was in business in 1711; there is a broadside with this imprint in the Harvard Collection.

BLARE, Josiah
BLARE, Elizabeth

J. Blare printed ballads and tales in black-letter, and his address was The Looking Glass on London Bridge.[1] There were also more substantial books, and the 3rd Edition of *The Progress of the Christian Pilgrim*, 1705, bears his imprint. When he died in 1706, his business was taken over by his widow, Elizabeth, and there was a Chancery action against her in 1707 over an infringement of the Stationers Company patent in almanacs. She published, probably in that same year, *The Andover Garland;* but it is not known when she went out of business.

BROOKS, S.

Brooks appears only as the partner of H. Woodgate (q.v.), circa 1760. Other details have been impossible to find.

BROOKSBY, Philip.
BROOKSBY, Elizabeth.

P. Brooksby was a well-known printer at the close of the seventeenth century. *God's Marvellous Wonders in England*, printed for P. Brooksby at The Golden Ball In Pye Corner, 1694, was one of the earliest chapbooks printed in Latin letters as opposed to the black-letter type which was still in use during the last decades of the seventeenth century. He was closely associated with other ballad printers, and appears to have printed few chapbooks. He died in 1696; and his wife Elizabeth took over the business until her death in 1703. Her last venture in publishing was probably *English Fortune Tellers* by John Philips, which appeared in that year. Brooksby addresses were The Ball in West Smithfield, The Golden Ball in West Smithfield and The Golden Harp and Ball in Pye Corner.

BROWN (E), C.

Two undated chapbooks in the Harvard Collection have this imprint; *Great Britain's Glory, being the History of King Arthur,* and *The Famous and Renowned History of the Nine Worthies of the World*. Brown was in business from 1682 until 1707.

CONYERS, G.

A chapbook, *The Garland of Good will,* "Printed for G. Conyers at the Sign of the Golden-ring, in Little Britain", is undated, but probably appeared in 1709 according to a catalogue of books at the end. In 1697 he had published, also from the Golden Ring, an edition of *The History of the Seven Wise Masters,* in black-letter. Conyers was a prolific printer of broadside ballads, and also published books on angling, astrology, building, cookery, medicine and other subjects.

CROWDER, S.

*The Whole Life and Merry Exploits of Bold Robin Hood* was published by Crowder at The Looking Glass on London Bridge in 1759 and he was at this address from about that time until 1770 when his premises were destroyed by fire. He was at one time associated with L. Hawes (q.v.) and C. Hitch (q.v.), and with J. King (q.v.); and for a short time he was apparently in partnership with H. Woodgate (q.v.), the firm being known as S. Crowder and Company. See also J. Hodges, whose apprentice he had been.

In 1775 he was in business again at The Golden Ball, Paternoster Row; and although amongst the many chapbooks which Crowder printed, editions of *Fortunatus* and *Guy of Warwick* were undated, it can be concluded (see J. Bew in this list) that at least the latter appeared after this date. Another of his titles was *Tommy Thumb's Little Song Book*, (ND), published from Paternoster Row. Crowder was a Wilkes supporter on the Court of Common Council 1768–1771. He died in 1798.

DICEY, W.
DICEY, C.
DICEY, T.
DICEY, R.

By far the largest number of chapbooks printed by a single firm during the eighteenth century came from one of the presses owned by the Dicey family, who had premises in London and Northampton. It was here that William Dicey, the founder, began printing chapbooks in the seventeen twenties; and before his death in 1756 his son, Cluer, was in business in London, first in Aldermary Church Yard, and later in Bow Church Yard where in 1761 a rate assessment shows that the business was occupying two houses. Cluer's son, Thomas, still used these premises in 1800, but by then the family owned a country mansion in Leicestershire. William Dicey's other son, Robert, died in 1757 while he was running the Northampton printing office.

The importance of the Diceys in the field of chapbook printing is very considerable. The immense range of their publications, already referred to, is shown also by the contents of a catalogue issued by them in 1754 of which The Bodleian Library has a copy. They used more than two dozen imprints upon their chapbooks at various times; none that I have examined is dated, but Dicey chapbooks are unmistakable. Many are preserved in the British Museum. Apart from sources already quoted, the following are useful:

Anon.    *History of the Northampton Mercury,* Northampton, 1901.

R. W.    *Northampton Printers,* etc., "Journal of the Northamp-
Brown    tonshire Natural History Society", Vol. 19, No. 156, December, 1918.

Northamptonshire Record Office Archives.

Second Register of All Saints, Northampton.

Guildhall (London) MS 5006/1.

Parish Registers of St. Mary le Bow, London, (Harleian Society Transcription, Vols. XLIV, XLV, 1914–1915).

DUTTON, J.

*A Terrible and Seasonable Warning to Young Men,* bearing the imprint of J. Dutton, near Fleet Street, is undated; while *The Constant Couple* is "Printed for J. D. near Fleet Street", and is dated 1709.

D., Mary.

The imprint "Printed and Sold by Mary D. at the Horse-shoe in Giltspur Street" is found upon a very popular chapbook, *Simple Simon's Misfortunes.* It is undated.

FOSTER, J.

Active at the beginning of the eighteenth century, and possibly during the last years of the seventeenth, his address being The Golden Ball in Pye Corner. An edition of *Reynard the Fox* was printed by W. Onley (q.v.), "and sold by J. Foster". He was also associated with G. Bates (q.v.), and in an undated edition of *Guy of Warwick* (circa 1700?) which was printed by "A. M." for them both, there is a list of books they issued, with the information that from their separate places of business "any country chapmen or others may be furnished with all sorts of historys, small books, and ballads, at reasonable rates". Both of these chapbooks are in the Harvard Collection.

G., H.

An undated chapbook *The Hop Garland* was "Printed for H.G."

HARRIS, T.

Bookseller and publisher at The Looking Glass on London Bridge, 1741-45. The date of his death is unknown.

HAWES, L.

At one time associated with S. Crowder (q.v.). A joint imprint with C. Hitch is on an undated edition of *Fortunatus* and on *The History of the Tales of the Fairies,* 1758; and an edition of *The Seven Champions of Christendom* was published by L. Hawes and Comp. in 1766. In 1758 C. Hitch and L. Hawes had premises at the Red Lyon in Paternoster Row.

HILLS, H.

Son of Henry Hills, King's Printer. *The Sailor's Warning Piece* was "Printed by H. Hills in Blackfryars". Although undated, it must have appeared in 1706 or 1707, since it describes the adventures of seven sailors who were shipwrecked in 1706. Another chapbook, *An Ode on the Incarnation,* was printed by Hills in 1709 "in Blackfryars, near the water-side". Hills died in 1713. There was also a P. Hills, but any relationship must be a matter of conjecture.

HINDE, A.

Hinde published *The Birth Parentage and Education, etc., of Mr. Christopher Slaughterford, Who was Executed at Guildford in Surrey* in 1709. In 1711 he published *The Whole Life and Conversation of that Foolish Creature called Granny.*

HITCH, C.

See S. Bates, S. Crowder, L. Hawes and J. Hodges.

HITCH, G.

(Relative of the above?). Associated with J. Hodges (q.v.) and A. Bettesworth (q.v.).

HODGES, J.

Bookseller, publisher who probably succeeded T. Norris (q.v.) at The Looking Glass on London Bridge, and was in business from circa 1732 to circa 1758.[2] In addition to chapbooks he published more substantial works, including the 6th Edition of *Winter Evenings Tales* in 1737, in which enterprise he was associated with A. Bettesworth (q.v.) and C. Hitch (q.v.). In the same year, together with J. Brotherton, W. Meadows, R. Ware and T. Astley, he published in three volumes the 3rd Edition of *A Collection of Novels and Tales of the Fairies.* From 1743 to 1744 Hodges was churchwarden of St. Magnus church, and in 1757 he was elected Town Clerk of the City of London. A contemporary account of the election describes him as "Mr. James Hodges, citizen and stationer," and in the following year, 1758, he was knighted by George II. There is a photographic reproduction of a portrait of Hodges by an unknown artist in the Guildhall Library. An edition of *Seven Wise Mistresses* dated 1754 shows Hodges and W. Johnston in association, while an undated *Dr. Faustus* shows him collaborating with A. Bettesworth (q.v.) and C. Hitch (q.v.). R. Ware (q.v.) was also concerned in this production, which contains an advertisement for books published by Ware and Hodges. At one time S. Crowder (q.v.) was an apprentice of Hodges. Hodges died in 1774 in Bath, and Timperly says of him that he was "many years a considerable bookseller (particularly in what were called Chap Books)". His imprint also appears on *The Muses Library* by Elizabeth Cooper, 1737, and *The Laboratory or School of Arts,* 2nd Edition, 1740.

HOLT, M.

The imprint "Printed by W. Wise and M. Holt in Fleet Street, 1708" occurs on a chapbook, *A Looking Glass for Swearers.*

HOW, L.

Larkin How, who had a printing office in Love Court, Petticoat Lane, published and sold a large number of chapbooks and broadsides. None of his productions seems to have been dated, but *Bibliotheca Lindesiana* quotes him as "circa 1780". I have come across none of his chapbooks in the British Museum; but the following is a list of those which he published, and which are in the Harvard Collection:

*The Gentle Craft*
*Dick Whittington*
*Robinson Crusoe*
*Robin Hood*
*Renowned Robin Hood*
*The Heathen's Conversion*
*The Life of Judas Iscariot*
*Fortunatus*
*Salus and Patient Grissel*
*Tom Thum*, Parts 1 and 2
*Tommy Pots* (see pp. 3 & 4, "A Catalogue of histories and merry books printed and sold by Larkin How").
*Tom Long the Carrier* (see p. 24, "A Catalogue of histories and merry books printed and sold by Larkin How").
*The Art of Courtship*
*The Second Part of Jack and the Giants* (see p. 24, "A Cata-. logue of histories and merry books printed and sold by Larkin How, in Petticoat Lane, London").

JOHNSTON, W.

At some time associated with James Hodges (q.v.). His address was The Golden Ball in St. Paul's Church Yard, and it was from here that he issued, with Hodges, *Seven Wise Mistresses* in 1754.

KING, J.

King was associated with C. Hitch (q.v.), L. Hawes (q.v.), and S. Crowder (q.v.) in an undated edition of *Fortunatus*. His address was given simply as Moorfields.

MARSHALL, J. (and Co.).
MARSHALL, R.

Many chapbooks were issued by one Marshall or another from "Aldermary Church Yard". In the history of publishing this name is something of a mystery. According to F. J. Harvey Darton, *Children's Books in England* 2nd Ed., Cambridge, 1958, John Marshall was in business at 4 Aldermary Church Yard in 1783. When he started in business there is not known, but not later than 1799 he had a shop in Cheapside, 17 Queen Street; while in 1800 he was in business at 140 Fleet Street, and the firm lasted until at least 1823. The Aldermary Church Yard address was, however, also retained. Earlier in the century, in 1708, another John Marshall was at The Bible in Grace-Church Street; while Joseph and William Marshall had premises at The Bible in Newgate Street from 1679 until at least 1725. From Grace-Church Street, John Marshall's advertisement announced that the trade -

"... may be furnished with all sorts of Chapmen's Books, Broadsides or Half-Sheets, and Lottery Pictures, As Birds,

Beasts, London Crys, etc., by the Gross or Dozen; also labels for Chyryrgeons Chests, Venice-Treacle Directions and Rappers, Hungary Directions, Bills, Funeral Tickets, Affidavits for Burials in Woollen, Receipts for Land Tax, etc., Wholesale or Retail, at the very lowest prices."[3]

In 1764 a Richard Marshall, in partnership with Cluer Dicey, issued a 120-page catalogue from the Printing Office in Aldermary Church Yard. It included the titles of 150 chapbooks. Whether Richard was related to John, and how long the partnership lasted, are matters for conjecture. The Dicey address was later Bow Church Yard, and as we have seen, there was a Marshall in Aldermary Church Yard at the close of the century. The relationships, if any, between the Marshalls, and why the partnership with Dicey was broken off, remain a mystery though Richard Marshall is named as a friend of Cluer Dicey in the latter's will.

## MIDWINTER, E.

A printer and bookseller at The Star, Pye Corner, who produced many chapbooks and ballads. In 1710 *The Northamptonshire Wonder* was printed and sold by Edward Midwinter. According to Plomer he ceased printing in 1725, but a chapbook, *A Guide from the Cradle to the Grave,* was printed and sold by E. Midwinter at the Three Crowns and Looking Glass in St. Paul's Church-yard in 1732. Thomas Gent, a noted printer of York (q.v. under "Provincial Printers — York") worked with Midwinter from about 1710 to 1713.

## NOON, J.

A chapbook, *Farther and More Terrible Warnings from God,* was printed by J. Noon, near Fleet Street, in 1708.

## NORRIS, T.

Norris was printing from 1695 until his death in 1732. Up to 1711 he was at St. Giles Without Cripplegate, and in that year he moved to the Looking Glass on London Bridge, where he took over premises which had been previously occupied by J. Blare (q.v.). From 1722 to 1723 Norris was churchwarden of St. Magnus on London Bridge; and he was described by another printer, Thomas Gent, as "a very rich bookseller on London Bridge whose country seat was at Holloway".

Besides many chapbooks and broadside ballads, Norris also printed nautical books. His imprint, together with that of R. Ware (q.v.) also appears on the second Edition of *The Spelling Dictionary* by Thomas Dyche, 1725. At the end there is a catalogue of Norris's publications, many of which are chapbooks. Norris also published William Stow's *Remarks on London* in 1722.

## ONLEY, W.

A printer in Little Britain and Bond's Stables near Chancery Lane from 1697 – 1709. He printed many chapbooks and broadside ballads, but these productions were seldom dated, and he frequently used his initials "W. O." as an imprint.

OSBORN, J.
See S. Bates.

PARSONS, J.
*The Story of Sarah Dorin* was published by J. Parsons in 1795.

PATEM, W.
*The Lawyer's Doom* was published for W. Patem in Fleet Street ND, but circa 1705. The subject matter is the case of Mr. Edward Jeffries, who was executed for murder in that year.

READ, J.
*The Distressed Child in the Wood; or the Cruel Unkle,* ND, was printed by J. Read behind the Green Dragon Tavern in Fleet Street. *The Devil upon Two Sticks* was printed by J. R. near Fleet Street in 1708. Read was in business from 1709 to 1724.

RHODES, H.
An undated edition of *The Gentle Craft* was printed for H. Rhodes at the Star, the corner of Bride-lane, Fleet-street. Rhodes was printing from 1681 to 1709.

SABINE, T.
Sabine issued many chapbooks, but none, so far as I am aware, was dated. Many of them are in the Harvard Collection. Some of his productions have the imprint "The London and Middlesex Printing Office"; others "T. Sabine"; while a few were issued by "T. Sabine and Son". On at least one occasion – an edition of *The Seven Wise Masters* – he collaborated with E. Sibley. In addition to chapbooks he published popular novels, a list of which, with synopses, is given in an 8-page catalogue at the end of *The History of Miss Sally Johnson.* The themes appear to be seduction, abduction and unhappy marriages. From the catalogues at the ends of several chapbooks it is clear that Sabine was a leading printer and publisher in the field of popular fiction. His address was 81 Shoe Lane, Holborn.

SAWYER, E.
*Rare Good News for Wives in City and Country* was printed for E. Sawyer in Gracious Street in 1706.

SAWBRIDGE, G.
SAWBRIDGE, H.
G. Sawbridge, who published many chapbooks from the Three Golden Fleur de Luces, Little Britain, also published scientific books. According to Plomer he was in business from 1692 until 1711, but *A Collection of Scarce and Valuable Papers* bears the imprint "George Sawbridge: London, 1712." H. Sawbridge was Hannah who, according to Plomer, was the widow of the G.

Sawbridge the elder who had died in 1681. There is no certainty that this was the case, and the problem is further complicated by the name "Tho. Sawbridge", who was in business in 1691. There is, however, no doubt that the names G. Sawbridge and H. Sawbridge appeared on chapbooks. In 1705 George Sawbridge published *The Traveller's and Chapman's Daily Instructor,* which was a guide to roads and fairs in England, printed for the use of those who travelled or who were itinerant merchants.

SIBLEY, E.
See T. Sabine.

SMITH, J.
*The French King's Wedding* was printed by J. Smith, near Fleet Street, in 1708; and *The Whole Tryal . . . of Madam Geneva* was printed by J. Smith in 1713.

SMITH, S.
*The Comical Bargain, or Trick upon Trick* was printed for S. Smith in Cornhil (sic) in 1707.

SYMPSON, C.
Printer and publisher of numerous chapbooks and broadsides towards the end of the eighteenth century. The address of the firm was Stonecutter Street, Fleet Market. Alternative imprints were "Sympson's" and "Sympson's Warehouse". An edition of *Divine Songs* by Isaac Watts published by W. and I. Sympson in 1778 indicates that this was a family business. Many Sympson productions are preserved in the Harvard Collection.

THORN, F.
There is an undated chapbook, *The Pleasant History of Taffy's Progress to London,* with the imprint: "London. Printed for F. Thorn near Fleet Street." Another edition is dated 1707.

TRACY, E.
An undated chapbook, *The Voyages and Travels of Sir Francis Drake*, was printed for E. Tracy at the Three Bibles on London Bridge.

TURPIN, H.
H. Turpin printed or sold an edition of *Nixon's Cheshire Prophecy* in 1784, and this included a list of children's books and other publications. He was in business from 1764 to 1787, and his address was The Golden Dog, West Smithfield.

WARE, R.
Printer or bookseller, apparently associated with James Hodges (q.v.), with whom a joint undated catalogue was issued. Ware also collaborated with Norris (q.v.) in the 2nd Edition of Thomas Dyche's *The Spelling Dictionary,* at the end of which there is a catalogue of Ware's books.

WATES, S.
*A Choice Pennyworth of Wit* was printed for S. Wates in Fleet Street, 1707.

WILLIAMS, T.
*The Horrors of Jealousie or the Fatal Mistake* was printed for T. Williams near Wood Street in 1707.

WISE, W.
Bookseller or printer associated with M. Holt (q.v.).

WOODGATE, H.
Bookseller and publisher at the Golden Ball in Paternoster Row. In partnership with S. Brooks (q.v.) he published many chapbooks and plays. The Rev. W. H. Dilworth, an historian, wrote several books for them, and a catalogue of chapbooks published by Woodgate and Brooks is printed at the end of Dilworth's *The Father of His Country,* 1760. It lists more than one hundred and fifty titles. At one time he was in partnership with S. Crowder (q.v.).

WYAT, J.
*The Guildford Ghost* was printed for J. Wyat in Southwark in 1709. This chapbook deals with a Mr. Christopher Slaughterford, who was the subject of a chapbook printed by A. Hinde (q.v.) in 1709.

1. There appear to have been two premises with this name on London Bridge. One was usually distinguished as "over against St. Magnus Church."
2. Plomer gives the date as circa 1730, but as Norris did not die until June, 1732, this is a more likely date.
3. The interest of this lies not only in its indication of the wide scope of Marshall's business, but also in the light it throws upon the printed material (other than books, broadsides, journals and pamphlets) with which folk would normally expect to be familiar at this early stage in the century.

## PRINTERS, PUBLISHERS AND BOOKSELLERS IN THE PROVINCIAL TOWNS OF ENGLAND.

[Listed under Towns in chronological order, with the object of indicating the development of provincial trade during the century]

The primary source for a study of the development of chapbook printing in the provincial towns of England in the eighteenth century is an examination of the chapbooks themselves, and we have seen that a substantial number of them has survived.

A valuable secondary source is the series of three articles by W. H. Allnutt which were published between 1879 and 1901:

(i) "Printers and Printing in the Provincial Towns of England and Wales", *Transactions and Proceedings of the First Annual Meeting of the Library Association of the United Kingdom*, Trubner, 1879, pp. 101–103, Appendix v, pp. 157–164.

(ii) "English Provincial Presses", *"Bibliographica"*, 3 Vols., 1895–97, Vol. II, pp. 276–308.

(iii) "Notes on the Introduction of Printing Presses Into the Smaller Towns of England and Wales to the End of the Eighteenth Century", *"The Library"*, New Series, Vol. II, 1901, pp. 242–259.

Other secondary sources include studies of printing in Newcastle and York, and articles on individual printers. These are mentioned under the towns concerned.

NEWCASTLE.

After London, Newcastle was the most important centre of chapbook production. In 1711, John White, son of the Royal Printer at York, set up a printing press in the Close, and in the following year he moved to his "House on the Side", where -

"... developing a special line in broadsides and booklets, he announced that chapmen could be furnished with sermons, histories and ballads, etc., and thither went peripatetic vendors of cheap literature for those treasuries of song, story and legend which formed the mental equipment of innumerable sons and daughters of toil throughout the northern counties."

White printed much material apart from chapbooks. Eight years before his death in 1769, he took into partnership Thomas Saint, and from 1761 to 1763 the business founded by White became known as "John White and Co.". In 1763, until White's death, it was called "John White and Thomas Saint"; and subsequently Saint, who was a noted printer of chapbooks, carried on the business in his own name until his death in 1788.

The other chapbook firm in Newcastle was founded in 1774 by Thomas Angus, and carried on after his death in 1787 by his widow, Margaret, who died in 1812. The business was then carried on for a time by her son, George Angus. The Angus chapbooks were well printed, sometimes upon grey-coloured paper, and the woodcut illustrations were occasionally coloured by hand.

Besides the imprints of White, Saint and Angus, a number of chapbooks were issued in Newcastle without either a printer's name or a date upon them.

YORK.

Thomas Gent[1] set up a press in Coffee Yard, York, in 1724, and from this address he issued many chapbooks. Before coming to York, Gent had worked in London with Edward Midwinter (q.v.). In 1717 Gent was a member of the Stationers' Company, but none of his London productions appears to have survived. Besides being a printer, he was also a writer, and amongst his works were histories of York, Ripon and Kingsgate. During the eighteenth century Thomas Gent was the leading printer of chapbooks in York. He died in 1778. For York printing generally there is a useful survey, *A Memoir of the York Press,* by Roland Davies (London, 1868).

### BIRMINGHAM.

E. Butler was printing chapbooks in Birmingham in about 1710, and an H. Butler was in business in about 1749. Other printers whose imprints are to be found on chapbooks are T. Holywell and J. Berry, circa 1769; Thomas Chapman, circa 1774; E. Jones, circa 1790; Swinney and Hawkins, circa 1799.

### NORTHAMPTON

William Dicey started printing chapbooks here in 1720 (see Dicey in the foregoing list).

### SHEFFIELD.

In about 1736 John Garnet was printing "at the Castle Green Head, near the Irish Cross. All sorts of New Songs and Penny Histories." He was still in business in 1744, printing for the Town Trustees. In 1752 he issued an edition of *The Blind Beggar of Bethnal Green.*

### WORCESTER.

S. Gamidge, printing between 1758 and 1768.

### TEWKESBURY.

S. Harward, a bookseller and printer, was at work from 1760 to 1809. He printed a large number of chapbooks, and a list of them was given in Bennett's *Tewkesbury Register and Magazine,* 1840-49, Vol. 2, pp. 191-2.

### LEICESTER.

Two chapbooks, *A Pleasant and Delightful Dialogue Between Honest John and Loving Kate,* and *An Excellent Dialogue Between Honest John and Loving Kate,* were printed at Leicester in about 1760. Neither has a printer's name on it. Plomer lists the names of six printers in Leicester, but there is no way of telling who published these chapbooks.

### BANBURY.

John Cheney commenced printing in 1767, and the firm of Cheney and Sons is still in existence. Until about 1820 a number of chapbooks were printed, but none of these seems to have been dated; and Cheney also sold chapbooks which he had not printed.

### NOTTINGHAM.

George Burbage commenced printing at 14 Long Row in about 1772. Many chapbooks were issued from his "Patter, Song and

History Warehouse", most of them undated, but a few quote dates of issue in 1779, 1792, 1794 and 1796. Burbage's obituary was printed in the *Nottingham Journal*, December 12th 1807, and it speaks of his having been in business for nearly sixty years. Charles Sutton, another chapbook printer in Nottingham, was in business in about 1794 in Bridlesmith Gate, and the firm continued in existence until 1871.

The foregoing details of Nottingham printers and chapbooks are to be found in an extremely scarce volume, Percy J. Cropper, *The Nottinghamshire Printed Chapbooks,* Nottingham, 1892. Only sixty copies were printed for sale, and until recently this book had been virtually forgotten.

CARLISLE.

Chapbooks were printed by F. Jolie and F. Jolie and Sons. One of them, *A True and Faithful Account of Christ's Coming to Judgement on the Last Day,* was printed by F. Jolie in 1770.

For an account of Carlisle printing the following should be consulted:

(i) R. S. Ferguson, "On the collection of chapbooks in the Bibliotheca Jacksoniana in Tullie House, Carlisle, with some remarks on the History of Printing in Carlisle, Whitehaven, Penrith And Other Northern Towns". Published in *Cumberland and Westmorland Antiquarian and Archaeological Society's Transactions,* Vol. 14, pp. 1—20, and Vol. 16, pp. 56—79, Kendal, 1897—1900.

(ii)R. S. Ferguson, "On the chapbooks in the Bibliotheca Jacksoniana in Tullie House, Carlisle". Published in the *Archeological Journal,* London, 1895, Vol. 52 (Series 2, Vol. 2), pp. 293—335.

See also WHITEHAVEN in this list.

COVENTRY.

John Turner, who was born in 1773, began printing in Coventry in about 1790. He issued chapbooks, which were undated, and a large number of broadside ballads.

MANCHESTER.

George Swindells had a printing office in Hanging Bridge during the last quarter of the eighteenth century. He issued chapbooks and broadsides, and on his death in 1796 the business was taken over by his son, who died in 1853. Swindells' chapbooks were of 16 pages, printed on coarse paper, and were usually illustrated with woodcuts. Samuel Bamford visited the premises and described them in his autobiography, *Early Days.*

DURHAM.

In about 1797 George Walker commenced a printing business, and part of his output consisted of chapbooks.

## WHITEHAVEN.

Several chapbooks were printed here at the end of the eighteenth century. They were issued by Alexander Coutts, who died in 1795; and John Dunn, who became a Customs Officer in 1778 – in this year his business was taken over by relatives, Browning N. Dunn and A. Dunn. A few chapbooks were also printed by Joseph Briscoe.

See also Carlisle in this list for notes of two articles on North Country printing by R. S. Ferguson.

## BATH.

The "Cheap Repository Tracts" were printed here by Samuel Hazard, who died in 1806.

## STOCKTON.

An unidated edition of *Youth's Warning-piece, or the Tragical History of George Barnwell* was printed at Stockton by an unidentified printer, probably at the end of the eighteenth century. Plomer gives J. Pickering as a bookseller in the town from 1763 to 1766, but does not mention that he was a printer. It seems very much more likely that this is the edition of *George Barnwell* which was printed and sold by R. Christopher of Stockton some time at the end of the century. This was a very popular chapbook, and was often reprinted. Christopher printed many children's chapbooks at the turn of the century.

Footnotes to 'Publishers and Booksellers in
the Provincial Towns of England'

1. For Thomas Gent, see: (i) *The Life of Mr. Thomas Gent, Printer, of York, Written by Himself*, London, 1832; (ii) C. A. Federer (Ed.), *Yorkshire Chapbooks*, 1st Series, London, 1889.

APPENDIX (iii)

## A STATISTICAL APPROACH TO LITERACY

A set of documents to which my attention was recently drawn in the Reference Library at Islington suggests that a statistical approach to one aspect of the problem of reading ability amongst the eighteenth century poor is possible.

In the parish of St. Mary, Islington, an *Annual register of the parish poor children until they are apprenticed out* was kept. Three volumes of the register have survived, covering the years 1767-1783; 1784-1799; 1800-1814. Amongst the information recorded was the ability or otherwise of the children to read; if they had this ability, the letter "r" was recorded in the appropriate column against the name.

This is clearly a valuable piece of contemporary evidence; but before it can be exploited effectively we need to know as precisely as possible what was meant by being a "reader". Eighteenth century theory and practice in elementary education[1] both point to the fact that ability of the poor to read was seen in terms of reading the Bible, or some possibly simplified devotional work. There can have been no objective method of ascertaining whether children coming into the care of the parish could do this; it is possible that they were given a portion of the Bible to read by the Parish official who was responsible for keeping records. They may simply have been asked whether they could read or not — and if so, did they answer for themselves or did parent or guardian speak for them? We have no means of knowing, but we can be reasonably certain that nothing beyond reading a simple religious passage, even haltingly perhaps, was expected.

The records were kept on a yearly basis. Each year the entries show all the children who were a charge upon the parish. This means that the same name may occur several years running. Accordingly, in extracting information I have counted the total number of children aged five or over, and those in this age range who were entered as able to read, in 1767 (the year for which this Islington register commences), and in subsequent years I have counted only the new entries aged over five, together with those of them who are shown as readers. With the exception of the years 1811 and 1814, when the record seems to have been maintained in an extremely perfunctory manner, the entries are for the most part clear and informative. A notable lapse occurs in 1772, when the clerk completely omitted any entries in the reading column — children from previous years who were shown as readers do not appear so in this one. The same thing occurred in 1808, and again during the last four years covered by the register, when the clerical work appears to have been unsatisfactory; indeed, in 1814 not even ages were shown, and upon only one other occasion, in 1770, was an age omitted. Several times children of four were shown as readers; these I have indicated, but not shown in the total for each year.

The following tables show the information recorded in these registers:

## TABLE ONE
### Parish poor children aged 5 or over in 1767

| No. of Children | Readers |
|:---:|:---:|
| 23 | 16 |

1. See Chapters 1 and 3 passim.

## TABLE TWO
New names of children aged 5 or over appearing in the register from 1768

| Year | No. of Children | Readers | Remarks |
|---|---|---|---|
| 1768 | 3 | — | |
| 1769 | 3 | 1 | |
| 1770 | 6 | 6 | |
| 1771 | 11 | 3 | |
| 1772 | 24 | — | Entries omitted? |
| 1773 | 4 | 4 | |
| 1774 | 10 | 7 | |
| 1775 | 2 | 2 | |
| 1776 | 4 | 2 | |
| 1777 | 10 | 9 | |
| 1778 | 10 | 9 | |
| 1779 | 10 | 10 | |
| 1780 | 10 | 9 | |
| 1781 | 9 | 8 | |
| 1782 | 11 | 7 | |
| 1783 | 24 | 16 | |
| 1784 | 4 | 3 | |
| 1785 | 8 | 5 | |
| 1786 | 6 | 6 | |
| 1787 | 5 | 5 | One 4-year old shown as reader |
| 1788 | 4 | 4 | |
| 1789 | 12 | 11 | |
| 1790 | 5 | 3 | |
| 1791 | 7 | 7 | |
| 1792 | 5 | 5 | |
| 1793 | 8 | 6 | |
| 1794 | 12 | 6 | |
| 1795 | 12 | 11 | |
| 1796 | 10 | 8 | |
| 1797 | 11 | 10 | |
| 1798 | 17 | 11 | |
| 1799 | 29 | 26 | |
| 1800 | 42 | 34 | |
| 1801 | 19 | 18 | |
| 1802 | 9 | 9 | |
| 1803 | 13 | 13 | |
| 1804 | 17 | 16 | Two 4-year olds shown as readers |
| 1805 | 12 | 10 | |
| 1806 | 11 | 11 | One 4-year old shown as reader |

| 1807 | 11 | 11 | One 4-year old shown as reader |
| 1808 | 22 | — | Some children shown as readers in previous years. |
| 1809 | 9 | 8 | |
| 1810 | 14 | 13 | |
| 1811 | 11 | — | No entries in |
| 1812 | 8 | — | the reader |
| 1813 | 8 | — | column for |
| 1814 | 3 | — | these years. |

## TABLE THREE

Combined number of Parish poor children from 1767 to 1810, with readers shown as totals of boys and girls, aged 5 or over, with percentages

| | Total | Readers | % |
|---|---|---|---|
| Boys | 267 | 205 | 74.5 |
| Girls | 228 | 173 | 75.7 |

To summarise these figures: very nearly five hundred children aged five or over appear on the list of Parish Poor Children between 1767 and 1810 when information about reading ability was (except for two years) entered in the Register. About three-quarters of the children are shown as readers, and there is no significant difference between boys and girls in this respect.

It seems reasonable to assume that most of these children came from the poorest section of the labouring class. A few might have been the offspring of failed shopkeepers or tradesmen, but the majority would be from distressed families, foundlings or illegitimate. The fact that three-quarters of them were able to read is an indication that those who initiated both Charity and Sunday Schools met with some degree of success in modifying the ignorance of the poor. As we know, facilities for elementary education were becoming widespread in the eighteenth century, and there existed a widely circulated cheap popular literature. These two factors are clearly connected with the fairly high incidence of reading ability amongst the least privileged members of society. We might perhaps infer that reading was at least no less widespread further up the social scale.

A caveat, however: these figures relate to only one parish, and it would be rash to draw from them conclusions which subsequent research might call in question. Moreover, such figures relate only to those poor children who were dependent upon the charity of the Parish. It is to be hoped that similar registers from other parts of the country have survived. An examination of them should provide a reliable statistical guide to literacy amongst destitute children in eighteenth century England; but whether we can go any further than this in statistics seems highly problematic.

# BIBLIOGRAPHY

Note

Unless otherwise stated in the Bibliography, the place of publication is London.

## SECTION A

### MANUSCRIPTS

| | |
|---|---|
| B. M. Add. MS 27,827, | Place Papers Vol. XXXIX. |
| B. M. Add. MS 35,142, | Place Papers Vol. LXXIII. |
| Guildhall Library MSS 75 & 75A | An Account of the Rise of the Society who Founded ye Charity School in Red Cross Street in the Parish of St. Giles's Without Cripplegate, London. |
| Guidhall Library MS 6999/1 | Aldersgate Ward School Minutes, 1748–1783. |
| Guildhall Library MS 7013/1 | Cripplegate Within Ward Schools Committee Minutes, 1712–1892. |
| Guildhall Library MS 9192/1 | St. Anne's School, Blackfriars, Minute Book, 1717–1787. |
| Guildhall Library MS 9445 | St. Sepulchre Holborn. Parochial Schools Boys School Subscribers and Trustee Minutes, 1740–87. |
| Guildhall Library MS 10219/1 | Castle Baynard Ward. Ward Schools Trustees Committee Minutes. |
| Guildhall Library MS 10,116 | Certificates of Schoolmasters, etc. |
| Bowyer-Bower, T. A. | The Development of Educational Ideas and Curricula in the Army during the 18th and 19th Centuries. |
| | Unpublished Thesis submitted to Nottingham University for the |

degree of M. Ed. in May, 1954. Copy in War Office Library.

Judson, S.,      Biographical and Descriptive Works on the Rev. John Wesley.

MS Bibliography submitted in part requirement for University of London Diploma in Librarianship (August, 1963). Copy in Methodist Archives.

Scott, G. K.,      English Public and Semi-Public Libraries in the Provinces, 1750–1850.

Unpublished essay in typescript submitted for the Library Association Final Examination, Part 6, July, 1951. (Possession of the author).

Scott, G. K.,      MS Notes on Library Stock of the 18th and early 19th Centuries. (Possession of the author).

Tydeman, S.,      The History of the Boys' Charity School of St. Sepulchre, London, c. 1750–1800, with reference to its beginnings from 1700 to 1750.

Unpublished essay. Typescript MS in Guildhall Library.

Wilson, J.,      The Journal of Sergeant John Wilson (15th Regiment of Foot), 1702–1711.

Unpublished MS in possession of the Duke of Northumberland. Written in 1736. Typescript in War Office Library.

Lee, Jesse,      A Memoir of Mr. John Collier.

Read at a meeting of the Manchester Literary and Philosophical Society, October 15th,

1839. Proof sheets with numerous MS additions by the author in Manchester Public Library.

## SECTION B

## COLLECTIONS

| | |
|---|---|
| Chapbook Collections, | British Museum. See General Catalogue, "COLLECTIONS". Press Marks: 1079 i 13 |
| | i 14 |
| | i 15 (3 Vols.) |
| | 1076 1 7 |
| | 1 1 |
| | 1 2 |
| | 1 24 |
| | (The above list is not exhaustive) |
| Chapbook Collections, | Bodleian Library. See "Douce Additions". |
| Lysons, D., | "Collectanea". 2 Vols. and 5 Vols. A collection of cuttings, etc., illustrating life in the 18th and early 19th centuries. (The British Museum). |
| Place, F., | "The Place Collection". Education: Vols. 33, 34, 57. |

NOTE:
There are also important chapbook collections in the Public Libraries of the larger provincial centres in England and Scotland.

## SECTION C

## PRINTED BOOKS UP TO 1799

| | |
|---|---|
| Anon., | *A representation of the present state of religion, with regard to* |

the late excessive growth of infidelity, heresy and profaneness, 1711.

Anon.,        *Education of young children and young students*, 2nd Edition, 1742.

Anon.,        *Methods used for erecting charity schools with the rules and orders by which they are governed*, 17th Edition, 1718.

Anon.,        *Proposals for the reformation of schools and universities, in order to the better education of youth; humbly offered to the serious consideration of the high court of parliament*, 1704.

Anon.,        *The tears of the press, with reflexions on the present state of England*, 1681.

Ash, J.,        *Sentiments on education collected from the best writers.* 2 Vols., 1777.

Belsham, T.,        *The importance of giving a proper education to the children of the poor*, 1791.

Bosanquet, M.,        *A letter to the Rev. Mr. John Wesley*, 1764.

Brokesby, F.,        *Of education*, 1701.

Butler, J. (Bishop of Bristol),        *A sermon preached in the parish church of Christ-Church, London: on Thursday May the 9th, 1745 .. to which is added an account of the Society for Promoting Christian 'Knowledge*, 1745.

Campbell, R.,        *The London Tradesman*, 1747.

Chapman, G.,        *A treatise on education.* 3rd Edition, Edinburgh, 1784.

Charke, Charlotte        *A narrative of the life of Mrs. Charlotte Charke*, 1755.

| | |
|---|---|
| Comenius, J. A., | *Orbis Pictus* (Trans. C. Hoole), 1705. |
| Dunton, J., | *The life and errors of John Dunton*, 1705. |
| Dykes, O., | *The Royal Marriage*, 1722. |
| Elphinston, J , | *Education, 1763.* |
| Evans, J. | *The palace of profitable pleasure*, 1621. |
| Evans, John (of Islington) | *An. essay on the education of youth*. 2nd Edition, ND (1799). |
| Glasse, S., | *A sermon preached before the President, Vice-Presidents, and Governors of the Marine Society, etc.*, 1778. |
| Green, T. | *Instructions for the poor*. 5th Edition, 1759. |
| Hadley, G., | *A new and complete history . . . of Kingston-Upon-Hull.* Kingston-Upon-Hull, 1788. |
| Hendley, W., | *A defence of the charity-schools*, 1735. |
| Hirst, William, | *The necessity and advantages of education*, 1728. |
| How, J., | *Some thoughts on the present state of printing and book-selling*, 1709. |
| Kinner, C., | *A continuation of Mr. John-Amos Comenius school endeavours, etc.*, ND (1648). |
| London, W., | *A catalogue of the most vendible books in England*, 1658. |
| Lowe, Solomon, | *The occasional critique on education*, 1728. |
| Lowe, Solomon, | *The Whetstone: a proposal of a new scheme of grammar, and method of instruction*, 1732. |
| Mandeville, Bernard de, | *The fable of the bees*, 1723; Second Part, 1728. |
| Manners, N., | *Some particulars of the life and experience of Nicholas Manners*, York, 1785. |

| | |
|---|---|
| Mason, J., | *Self-Knowledge. A Treatise, showing the Nature and Benefit of that Important Science, and the way to attain it, 1745.* |
| Meres, F., | *Palladis Tamia, wits treasury. Being the Second Part of Wits Commonwealth, 1598.* |
| Mitchell, T., | *A short account of the life, trials and deliverances of Thomas Mitchell.* Leeds, 1784. |
| Monro, G., | *An essay upon Christian education, 1712.* |
| Negus, T., | *A sermon preached in the parish-church of Christ-Church London, on Thursday May the 14th, 1761, 1761.* |
| Nelson, J., | *An essay on the government of children, 1756.* |
| Nelson, J., | *The case of John Nelson. Written by himself.* 2nd Edition, 1745. |
| Olivers, T. | *An account of the life of Mr. Thomas Olivers. Written by himself, 1779.* |
| Pawson, J. & Mather, A., | *An affectionate address to the members of Methodist societies, 1796.* |
| Petty, William | *The advice of W. P. to Mr. Samuel Hartlib, for the advancement of some particular parts of learning, 1648.* |
| Postlethwayt, M. | *The merchant's public counting-house: or new mercantile institution: wherein is shewn, the Necessity of young Merchants being bred to the trade with greater Advantages than they usually are, 1750.* |
| Rogers, J., | *A short account of Mr. James Rogers. Written by himself, 1792.* |

| | |
|---|---|
| Simes, Thomas (Captain) | *The military medley.* Dublin, 1767. |
| Snell, G., | *The right teaching of useful knowledg,* 1649. |
| Spence, J., | *A full and authentick account of Stephen Duck the Wiltshire poet,* 1731. |
| Talbott, J., | *The Christian school-master,* 1707. |
| Taylor, T., | *Redeeming Grace displayed to the chief of sinners. Being a short Account of God's dealings with Thomas Taylor.* 3rd Edition, Leeds, 1781. |
| Tryon, T., | *A new method of educating children,* 1695. |
| Ward, Ned, | *The London spy,* 1700. |
| Wase, C., | *Considerations concerning free-schools as settled in England.* Oxford, 1678. |
| Watts, I., | *A discourse on the way of instruction by Catechism and the best manner of composing them.* 3rd Edition (Corrected), 1736. |
| Watts, I., | *An essay against uncharitableness,* 1707. |
| Watts, I., | *An essay towards the encouragement of charity schools,* 1728. |
| Watts, I., | *The improvement of the mind.* 2 Vols., 1782. (First published 1741). |
| Watts, Thomas, | *An essay on the proper method for forming the man of business.* 4th Edition, 1722. |
| Wilton, T. (Bishop of Sodor and Man) | *The principles and duties of Christianity . . . to which is now prefixed the true Christian method of educating the children of the rich and the poor.* 5th Edition, 1736. |

| | |
|---|---|
| Wolfe, J., | *General Wolfe's instructions to young officers: also his orders for a battalion and an army,* 1768. |

## SECTION D

## PRINTED BOOKS AND ARTICLES FROM 1800

| | |
|---|---|
| Adamson, J. W., | *Pioneers of modern education, 1600-1700,* Cambridge, 1921. |
| Adamson, J. W., | *The illiterate Anglo-Saxon,* Cambridge, 1946. |
| Allen, W. O. B. & McClure, E., | *Two hundred years: The history of the society for promoting Christian knowledge,* 1698-1898, 1898. |
| Altick, R. D., | *The English common reader. A Social History of the Mass Reading Public 1800–1900,* University of Chicago Press, 1957. |
| Anders, H., | *The Elizabethan ABC with the Catechism,* 1935. |
| Anderson, W., | *Self-made men,* 2nd Edition, 1865. |
| Anon., | *An address on religious tract distribution, with a word to the distributors,* ND (circa 1830) |
| Anon., | *Notes and sketches illustrative of northern rural life in the eighteenth century,* Edinburgh, 1877. |
| Anon., | *Self-taught men: a series of biographies,* 1878. |
| Armytage, W. H. G., | *Four hundred years of English education,* 1964. |
| Ashton, John, | *Chap-books of the eighteenth century,* 1882. |

Ashton, John,      *Social life in the reign of Queen Anne.* A New Edition, 1883.

Ashton, T. S.,      *Changes in standards of comfort in eighteenth century England.* The Raleigh Lecture on History, British Academy, 1955. From The Proceedings of the British Academy, Vol. XLI.

Baker, W. P.,      *Parish registers and illiteracy in East Yorkshire,* East Yorkshire Local History Society, 1961.

Bamford, S.,      *Early days,* 1840.

Bantock, G. H.      *The implications of literacy.* An Inaugural Lecture, Leicester, 1966.

Bell, Vicars,      *To meet Mr. Ellis. Little Gaddesden in the Eighteenth Century,* 1956.

Bett, H.,      *The alleged illiteracy of early Methodist preachers.* Proceedings of the Wesley Historical Society, Vol. XV, 1926, pp. 85–92.

Binns, J.,      *Recollections of the life of John Binns, Written by himself,* Philadelphia, 1854.

Birchenough, C.,      *History of elementary education in England & Wales,* 2nd Ed., 5th Impression, 1930.

Blacket, J.,      *The remains of Joseph Blacket ... and a memoir of his life by Mr. Pratt,* 2 Vols., 1811.

Blagden, C.,      *Notes on the ballad market in the second half of the seventeenth century.* Papers of the Bibliographical Society of the University of Virginia, Vol. 6, 1953–54.

Blakey, D.,     *The Minerva Press, 1790-1820.* The Bibliographical Society, 1939.

Blencowe, R. W. (Ed.),     *Extracts from the journal of Walter Gale, schoolmaster at Mayfield, 1750.* Sussex Archaeological Collections, Vol. IX, 1857.

Blunden, E., (Ed.),     *Sketches in the life of John Clare by himself,* 1931.

Bobbin, T. (John Collier),     *The miscellaneous works of Tim Bobbin, etc., to which is added a life of the author,* Salford, 1811.

Bowden, W.,     *Industrial society in England towards the end of the eighteenth century,* 2nd Edition, 1965.

Bready, J. W.,     *England before and after Wesley,* 1938.

Britton, John,     *The auto-biography of John Britton,* F.S.A., Part 1. "Printed for the Author", 1850.

Cardwell, Rev. J. H.,     *The story of a charity school,* 1899.

Carter, Thomas,     *Memoirs of a working man,* 1845.

Charlton, K.,     *Education in renaissance England,* 1965.

Clarke, W. K. Lowther,     *Eighteenth century piety,* S. P. C. K., 1945.

Cole, G. D. H.,     *A short history of the British working-class movement, 1789–1947,* 1952.

Collins, A. S.,     *Authorship in the days of Johnson,* 1927.

Compton, H. F. B.,     *Thomas Coram,* S.P.C.K., 1918.

Conway, M. D.,     *The life of Thomas Paine,* 1909.

Cozens-Hardy, B.,     *The diary of Sylas Neville, 1767-1788,* 1950.

Cragg, G. R., *The church and the age of reason,* 1960.

Craik, G L., *The pursuit of knowledge under difficulties,* 2 Vols., 1830–31.

Crane, R.S., *The vogue of "Guy of Warwick" from the close of the middle ages to the romantic revival.* Publications of the Modern Language Association of America, Vol. XXX. 2 (New Series, Vol. XXXIII. 2), 1915, pp. 125–194.

Cranfield, G.A., *The development of the provincial newspaper, 1700-1760* Oxford, 1962.

Crawfurd, Rev. G.P. (Ed.), *The diary of George Booth of Chester and Katherine Howard, his daughter, of Boughton, near Chester, 1707–1764,* Chester, 1928.

Crowther, J., *An apology for the liberty of the press among the Methodists,* 2nd Edition, Halifax, 1810.

Cumbers, F., *The book room,* 1956.

Dalziel, M., *Popular fiction 100 years ago,* 1957.

Davis, D., *A history of shopping,* 1966.

Davies, R., *A memoir of the York Press,* 1868.

Defoe, D., *A tour through England and Wales,* with an Introduction by G. D. H. Cole, 2 Vols., Everyman's Library, ND.

Dickson, A., *Valentine and Orson,* New York, 1929.

Dobbs, A. E.,      *Education and social movements, 1700-1850*, 1919.

Downing, J.,      *A narrative of the life of James Downing (a blind man), late a private in His Majesty's 20th Regiment of foot*, 6th Edition, 1818.

Drew, S.,      *The life, character and literary labours of Samuel Drew, A. M. By His Eldest Son*, 1834.

Dunlop, J. C.,      *The history of fiction*, 3 Vols., 1814.

Eastman, P. M.,      *Robert Raikes and Northamptonshire Sunday schools*, London & Northampton, 1880.

Ernle, Lord,      *The light reading of our ancestors*, 1927.

Evans, J.,      *The importance of educating the poor*, 2nd Edition, Canterbury, 1808.

Fish, H.,      *Memoirs of Joseph Pearson*, 1849.

Fison, Mrs. W.,      *Colportage: its history and relation to home and foreign Evangelization*, 1859.

Fowler, J. (Ed.),      *The life and literary remains of Charles Reece Pemberton*, 1843.

Furnivall, F. J.,      *Captain Cox, his ballads and books*, 1871.

Fussell, G. E.,      *The English rural labourer*, 1949.

George, M. D.,      *England in transition*, 1962.

George, M. D.,      *London life in the XVIIIth century*, 2nd Impression, 1925.

Gilboy, E. W.,      *Wages in eighteenth century England*, Harvard University Press, 1934.

Gonzales, Don Manoel      *London in 1731*, 1894.

Greenwood, C.,      *A report upon the property and income of the Christ Church*

| | |
|---|---|
| | *Southwark, parochial school trust . . . together with a Brief Historical Account of the Schools and Parish of Christ Church from the year 1707 to 1888,* 1888. |
| Hackwood, F. W., | *William Hone his life and times,* 1912. |
| Halliwell, J. O., | *Some account of a collection of several thousand bills, accounts and inventories, Illustrating the History of Prices Between the Years 1650 and 1750,* 80 copies Privately Printed, 1852. |
| Handover, P. M., | *Printing in London,* 1960. |
| Hans, N., | *New trends in education in the eighteenth century,* 1951. |
| Harben, H. A., | *A dictionary of London,* 1918. |
| Harrison, J. F. C., | *Learning and living 1790-1960,* 1961. |
| Hart, A. Tindal, | *Country counting house,* 1962. |
| Hazlitt, W. C., | *Old English jest-books,* 3 Vols., New York, ND (1964). |
| Hedderwick, R. G., | *The story of self-made men,* 2nd Edition, ND (circa 1890?). |
| Herford, C. H., | *Studies in the literary relations of England and Germany in the sixteenth century,* Cambridge, 1886. |
| Hewitt, G., | *Let the people read,* 1949. |
| Holcroft, T., | *Memoirs of Thomas Holcroft.* Written by himself and continued by William Hazlitt, 3 Vols., 1816, reprint in 1 Vol., Oxford, 1926. |
| Howitt, W., | *The rural life of England,* 2nd Edition, 1840. |
| Hudson, J. W., | *The history of adult education,* 1851. |
| Humphreys, A. R., | *The Augustan world,* 1954. |

| Hutton, W., | *The life of William Hutton, F.A.S.S.*, written by himself . . . 1816. |
| Hutton, W., (Ed. Llewellynn Jewitt) | *The life of William Hutton, and the history of the Hutton family.* ND (circa 1880). |
| Johnston, A., | *Enchanted ground.* The Study of Medieval Romance in the Eighteenth Century, 1964. |
| Jones, M. G., | *The charity school movement*, 1964. |
| Jusserand, J. J. | *The English novel in the time of Shakespeare.* Revised and Enlarged by the Author, 1908. |
| Kelly, Thomas, | *A history of adult education in Britain*, Liverpool, 1962. |
| Kelly, Thomas, | *Adult education in Liverpool.* A Narrative of two hundred years, Liverpool, 1960. |
| Kendall, G., | *Robert Raikes*, 1939. |
| Knight, C., | *The old printer and the modern press*, 1834. |
| Knight, C., | *Passages of a working life*, 3 Vols., 1864-65. |
| Knight, C., | *Once upon a time*, 1865. |
| Lackington, J., | *Memoirs of the forty-five first years of the life of J. Lackington, bookseller, Finsbury-Square, London, etc.*, 1803. |
| Lamb, R., | *Memoir of his own life*, Dublin, 1811. |
| Laslett, P., | *The world we have lost*, 1965. |
| Law, William, | *A serious call to a devout and holy life*, 18th Edition, 1816. |
| Lawson, J., | *Primary education in East Yorkshire, 1560-1902,* East Yorkshire Local History Society, 1959. |
| Leader, R. E., | *Sheffield in the eighteenth century*, Sheffield, 1901. |

| | |
|---|---|
| Leavis, Q. D., | *Fiction and the reading public*, 1932 (Reprint 1965). |
| Lewis, M. M., | *Language in society*, 1947. |
| Lewis, M. M., | *The importance of illiteracy*, 1953. |
| Linton, W. J., | *James Watson A memoir*, Appledore Private Press, 1879. |
| Love, David, | *The life, adventures and experiences of David Love, written by himself*, 3rd Edition, Nottingham, 1823. |
| Lovett, W., | *The life and struggles of William Lovett*, 1876. |
| Lowenthal, L., | *An historical preface to the popular culture debate*, Published in "Culture for the Millions", Ed. Norman Jacobs, Beacon Press, Boston, U. S. A., 1964, pp. 28—42. |
| Lowenthal, L., & Fiske, M., | *The debate over art and popular culture in eighteenth century England.* Essay published in "Common Frontiers of the Social Sciences", Ed. M. Komarovsky, The Free Press, Glencoe, Illinois, 1957. |
| Mantoux, Paul, | *The industrial revolution in the eighteenth century*, 1964. |
| Marshall, Dorothy, | *English people in the eighteenth century*, 1956. |
| Mason, M. G., | *The history of elementary education on Tyneside before 1870*, "Research Review" No. 2, September, 1951. The Research Publication of the Institute of Education, University of Durham. |
| Mathews, H. F., | *Methodism and the education of the people 1791-1851*, 1949. |
| Moffitt, L., | *England on the eve of the industrial revolution*, 1963. |

Moritz, Carl Philip, (Trans. and Ed. Reginald Nettel) — *Journeys of a German in England in 1782*, 1965.

Morton, A. L., & Tate, G., *The British Labour Movement*, 1956.

McClure, Rev. E., *A chapter in English church history*, 1888.

Neuburg, V. E., *The penny histories*, Oxford, 1968.

Owen, David, *English philanthropy 1660-1960*, Oxford, 1965.

Pinks, W. J., *The history of Clerkenwell*, 1865.

Pixell, Rev. J. V., *A short history of the hamlet of Ratchiff school founded 1710*, 1910.

Place, Francis, *Improvement of the working people. Drunkenness — Education*, 1834.

Plomer, H. R., *The booksellers of London Bridge*, Article in "The Library", New Series, Vol. IV, 1903, pp. 28–46.

Plomer, H. R., *The Church of St. Magnus and the booksellers of London Bridge*, Article in "The Library", Third Series, Vol. II, 1911, pp. 384–395.

Pole, T., *An address to the committee of the Bristol society for teaching the adult poor to read the Holy Scriptures*, Bristol, 1813.

Pole, T., *A history of the origin and progress of adult schools*, 2nd Edition, Bristol, 1816.

Pottle, F. A., *Boswell's London journal, 1762-63*, 1950.

Pritchard, M., *The meeting house at Newington Green*, No publisher's imprint. Bicentenary Souvenir Pamphlet, 1908.

| | |
|---|---|
| Rees, A. J., | *Old Sussex and her diarists*, 1929. |
| Reid, W. H., | *The rise and dissolution of the infidel societies in this metropolis*, 1800. |
| Routh, H. V., | *The advent of modern thought in popular literature*, (Ch. XVI, The Cambridge History of English Literature) Cambridge, 1911. |
| Salmon, D., | *The education of the poor in the eighteenth century*, Educational Record, October, 1907, pp. 369—387; February, 1908, pp. 495—512. |
| Sangster, P., | *Pity my simplicity*, The Evangelical Revival and the Religious Education of Children, 1738—1800, 1963. |
| Saussure, C, de (Trans. and Ed. Madame van Muyden), | *A foreign view of England in the reigns of George I and George II*, 1902. |
| Schlauch, M., | *Antecedents of the English novel, 1400-1600*, Warsaw, 1963. |
| Silver, H., | *The concept of popular education*, 1965. |
| Simon, B., | *Studies in the history of education, 1780-1870*, 1960. |
| *Simon, J. S.*, | *The revival of religion in the eighteenth century*, ND (1907). |
| Simpson, D., | *A plea for religion*, 2nd Edition, 1803. |
| Sjoberg, G., | *The preindustrial city*, New York, 1965. |
| Smith, F., | *A history of English elementary education, 1760-1902*, 1931. |
| Spence, L., | *A dictionary of medieval romance and romance writers*, 1913. |

Stephen, Leslie,      *English literature and society in the eighteenth century*, (First published 1904) 1963.

Stephen, Leslie,      *History of English thought in the eighteenth century*, 2 Vols., 1876.

Stephen, Leslie,      *The English utilitarians*, 3 Vols. Vol. i, 1900.

Stevenson, G. J.,      *City Road Chapel London and its associations. Historical, biographical and memorial*, ND (1872).

Stromberg, R.,      *Religious liberalism in eighteenth century England*, Oxford, 1954.

Strutt, J.,      *The sports and pastimes of the people of England*, 1838.

Sturge, C. Y. (Ed.)      *Leaves from the past. The diary of John Allen . . . written between February and July, 1777*, Bristol, 1905.

Sugden, E. H.,      *John Wesley's London*, 1932.

Sutherland, J.,      *A preface to eighteenth century poetry*, Oxford, 1948.

Tate, W. E.,      *The parish chest*, Cambridge, 1960.

Thompson, E. P.,      *The making of the English working class*, 1963.

Thompson, E. P.,      *Working-class culture. The transition to industrialism.* Article in Bulletin No. 9 Autumn, 1964) of The Society for the Study of Labour History.

Thompson, J. W.,      *The literacy of the laity in the middle ages*, New York, 1963.

Todd, William (Ed. C. T. Atkinson),      *A soldier's diary of the seven years war*, Journal of The Society for Army Historical Research, Vol. XIX, Nos. 119 & 120, Autumn and Winter, 1951.

| | |
|---|---|
| Told, Silas, | *The life of Mr. Silas Told, written by himself.* (First published 1786) 1954. |
| Tompkins, J. M. S., | *The popular novel in England, 1770-1800,* 1932. |
| Tuer, A. W., | *The history of the horn book,* 2 Vols., 1896. |
| Turberville, A. S., | *English men and manners in the 18th century,* New York, 1961. |
| Turberville, A. S. (Ed.), | *Johnson's England,* 2 Vols., Oxford, 1933. |
| Turnbull, G. H., | *Hartlib, Dury and Comenius,* Liverpool, 1947. |
| Turner, Thomas (Ed. F. M. Turner) | *The diary of Thomas Turner of East Hoathly (1754-1765),* 1925. |
| Wale, H. J., | *My Grandfather's pocket-book,* 1883. |
| Wallas, G., | *The life of Francis Place,* 1918. |
| Warner, W. J., | *The Wesleyan movement in the industrial revolution,* 1930. |
| Wasserman, E. R., | *Elizabethan poetry in the eighteenth century,* pp. 253–259, Illinois, 1947. |
| Watson, J., | Supplement to *The reasoner,* No. 402, Sunday, Feb. 5, 1854. A 16 pp. supplement presented gratis with this number of "The Reasoner". |
| Watt, I., | *The rise of the novel,* 1957. |
| Wearmouth, R. F., | *Methodism and the common people of the eighteenth century,* 1945. |
| Webb, R. K., | *The British working class reader, 1790-1848,* 1955. |
| Weber, H., | *Metrical romances of the thirteenth, fourteenth and fifteenth centuries,* 3 Vols., Edinburgh, 1810. |
| Weiss, Harry B., | *A book about chapbooks,* Trenton, New Jersey, 1942. |

| | |
|---|---|
| Welford, R., | *Early Newcastle typography*, Newcastle, 1906. |
| Wesley, J. (Ed. N. Curnock) | *The journal of John Wesley*, 8 Vols., 1909-16. |
| Whiteley, J. H., | *Wesley's England*, 4th Edition, 1954. |
| Willey, Basil, | *The eighteenth century background*, Published 1940, 8th Impression 1965. |
| Williams, Basil., | *The whig supremacy, 1714-1750*, 2nd Edition, Revised by C. H. Stuart, Oxford, 1962. |
| Winks, W. E., | *Lives of illustrious shoemakers*, 1883. |
| Woodforde, J., | *The diary of a country parson*, 5 Vols., 1924-31. |
| Wright, L. B., | *Middle class culture in Elizabethan England*, Cornell University Press, 1958. |
| Wright, T., | *England under the house of Hanover*, 2 Vols., 3rd Edition, 1849. |
| Wrigley, E. A. (Ed.) | *An introduction to English historical demography*, 1966. |
| Wroot, H. E., | *A pioneer in cheap literature. William Milner of Halifax.* The Bookman, March, 1897, pp. 169-175. |

## SECTION E

## BIBLIOGRAPHIES

| | |
|---|---|
| Alston, R. C., | *A bibliography of the English language from the invention of printing to the year 1800*, Vol. Four, Spelling Books, Bradford, 1967. |

Anon.,                    *Life in the ranks, 1642-1792.* War Office Library Book List 916 (Single sheet, duplicated), April, 1959.

Anon.,                    *Life in the ranks, 1792-1815.* War Office Library Book List 917 (2 sheets, 3 pp., duplicated), 4th Issue, September, 1961.

Fordham, Sir G. H.,      *The road books and itineraries of Great Britain, 1570 to 1850.* A Catalogue with an Introduction and a Bibliography. Cambridge, 1924.

Green, R.,               *The works of John and Charles Wesley.* A Bibliography, 2nd Edition, 1906.

Guildhall Library,       *London rate assessments and inhabitants lists in Guildhall library and the Corporation of London records office.* The Library Committee, Corporation of London, 1961.

Halliwell, J. O.,        *A catalogue of chap-books, garlands, and popular histories in the possession of James Orchard Halliwell, Esq.,* Privately Printed, 1849.

Halliwell, J. O.,        *Some account of a singular and unique collection of early penny merriments and histories. Printed at Glasgow, 1695—8. In the possession of J. O. Halliwell,* 25 copies, Printed for the Editor, 1864.

Higson, C. W. J.,        *Sources for the history of education,* 1967.

Kelly, Thomas (Ed.),     *A select bibliography of adult education in Great Britain,* 1952.

Kennedy, A. G.,      *A bibliography of writings on the English Language*, Harvard, 1927.

Lane, W. Coolidge, (Ed.),    *Catalogue of English and American chap-books and broadsides in Harvard College Library*, Cambridge, Mass., 1905.

Lemon, R.,      *Catalogue of a collection of printed broadsides in the possession of the Society of Antiquaries of London*, 1866.

Mattews, William,      *Bristish diaries. An annotated bibliography of British diaries written between 1442 and 1942*, California, 1950.

McBurney, W. H.,      *A check list of English prose fiction, 1700-1739*, Harvard, 1960.

Neuburg, V. E.,      *Chapbooks: a bibliography of references to English and American chapbook literature of the eighteenth and nineteenth centuries*, 1964.

Pargellis, S., & Medley, D. J.,      *Bibliography of British history of the eighteenth century, 1714-1789*, Oxford, 1951.

Weiss, Harry B.,      *A catalogue of the chapbooks in the New York Public Library*, New York, 1936.

# INDEX